BARE KNUCKLE SELLING

KNOCKOUT SALES TACTICS THEY WON'T TEACH YOU AT BUSINESS SCHOOL

SIMON HAZELDINE

LEANMARKETING™
★PRESS★

First Published In Great Britain 2005
by Lean Marketing Press
www.BookShaker.com

Typeset in Trebuchet

For KP & TJ
Who don't need to read this book!

Contents

Acknowledgements

Before we get started I'd just like to thank...

My wife Karen for her continued support   and endless proof reading!

My son Thomas who demonstrates his ability to be highly influential on a daily basis.

My NLP trainers – Jo Cooper and Peter Seal from Centre NLP (www.cnlp.com) for teaching me 'the real stuff'.

All of my fellow NLP explorers, in particular Sian Livesey from Beaumont Resource Development, Julie French from the Academy of High Achievers (www.aha success.com) and Jamie Smart from Salad (www.saladltd.co.uk).

Joe and Debbie at Lean Marketing Press (www.bookshaker.com) for their enthusiasm and support.

Nigel Percy (www.tibidi.info & www.nigelpercy.co.uk) for the many wonderful "You Can If You Think You Can" experiences we have shared.

Gary Outrageous (www.garyoutrageous.com) for showing me the power of networking.

Dr Hadyn Ingram for many years of academic support and challenge.

The many customers whom I've sold to over the course of my sales career.

All of the sales people that I have managed, led, trained and coached. I have learnt more from you than you have from me!

Foreword

Let's take off the gloves.

Let's get in the street.

Let's do business where the rules don't matter: In the real world.

After all, isn't there where all the selling takes place?

Selling doesn't take place in a lab. Or in a class room. Or in a weekend seminar where everything is controlled. Selling   real world selling   takes place in *real* time, with *real* people, in *real* situations.

If you don't know how to street fight in the raw world of right now reality, you won't sell anything to anybody.

And you and your family will starve.

Thank goodness this book is in your hands. Once you absorb the principles and methods in it, you'll have the skills integrated within you to do battle in the streets and make the cash register ring loud and clear.

You won't actually be fighting anyone, of course. But you'll be winning in the game of life where the only thing that counts is the thing you want the most: the sale.

Read this book. Become one with this book. Share it with coworkers (but not your competition).

And then go out and profit.

Expect miracles.

Dr. Joe Vitale
Author of way too many books to list here
www.MrFire.com

Preface

Hello and welcome to the wonderful world of selling!

"The wonderful world of selling!" I hear you cry in disbelief. "What is so wonderful about selling these days? It's tough out there!" I hear you moan. "And it's getting more competitive and cut throat every day! People are far better informed, and they can spot a sales pitch a mile off!"

I didn't say that selling isn't challenging at times. I didn't say that the modern commercial world isn't tough sometimes. What I am saying is that selling does not have to be that difficult. Far too many people make the process of selling very difficult for themselves. They follow the herd, and use the same worn out techniques that they have seen most other sales people use – whether effective or not.

Unfortunately, for people using these selling approaches, times have changed and they just don't work anymore – if they ever really did. You need to stop following the herd and *use what really works*.

If you are looking for a guaranteed way to improve your sales in a demanding commercial world then here it is: If you want to improve your sales rate then you have to improve your selling ability. It's that simple. The good news is that you *can* improve your selling ability. Bare Knuckle Selling is going to help you to do just that!

So why write a book entitled Bare Knuckle Selling? Bare knuckle fighters have to strip down various fighting techniques and only use what really works. In a bare knuckle fight there is no room for flashy techniques and showmanship. In the same way, Bare Knuckle Sellers use only the hard hitting selling techniques. They use simple, effective and efficient techniques that have been stripped back to *what really works*. They use these techniques to beat their competitors.

Bare Knuckle Selling has been created by brutally stripping all the mystery out of the selling process (and there is a vitally important process that you *must* follow if you want to sell successfully) back to what really works. Bare Knuckle Selling is a highly effective, street tested, selling process that will enable you to sell more, to more people, more often. And it will make the whole process far easier and far more rewarding.

Bare Knuckle Selling is not just a theoretical model dreamt up in an ivory tower. It has been developed from years of hard won experience, pounding the pavement, beating the competition and winning the respect of the customer. Every single element of the process is tried and tested and proven to ensure you get what you want – more sales and very happy customers.

It is a simple, logical and highly effective process that is easy to follow. Perhaps the most important thing about Bare Knuckle Selling is that the customer is the most important person. Your customers will love the Bare Knuckle Selling process. In fact they won't think they have been sold to. They will think that they have made a wise decision to buy!

Your customer will be right. When a customer buys something as a result of the Bare Knuckle Selling process you can be certain that they will be delighted with it. That means you get happy customers. Happy customers buy from you again and again. They will also recommend you to their contacts, friends and acquaintances. This means more sales for you. This is the wonderful world of selling! A world that is exciting and satisfying. The only people who won't like Bare Knuckle Selling are your competitors!

Good Luck and Good Selling!

Simon Hazeldine, MSc, FInstSMM
August 2005

Selling Makes The World Go Round

If you ask the average man or woman on the street to describe a salesperson, what do you think they would say? "Slimy", "Rip off merchant", "Shyster", "Con Artist", "Pushy", "Fast talking", "Flashy", "Manipulative", "Snake oil salesman", "Dave the dodgy double glazing guy", "Arthur Daley style used car merchants", "Liars", "Deceitful" – and they're just the more polite comments!

With that stereotype floating around our society, is it any wonder that the world of selling is regarded with suspicion?

I am prepared to place a bet that very few people reading this book were encouraged by their parents to pursue a career in selling! It is not exactly the career most parents have in mind for their children.

Be a doctor, solicitor, manager, shop assistant, perhaps even a bank robber but not a salesperson! Is it any wonder that parents would feel like this with the stereotypical salesperson being so mistrusted?

So, if selling isn't top of most people's career choices then how do people become sales people? Perhaps people end up in selling because they just aren't good at anything else. Perhaps selling is what you do if you can't find a 'proper job'.

After all who would choose to manipulate people for a living?

This erroneous view of sales people annoys me. I am not surprised by it, just annoyed by it. And why do people have this view of sales people? Because in many cases, it is true! There are just too many sales people who use manipulative tactics. There are too many commission hungry bandits in the field. So, is it any wonder that people are suspicious of sales people?

But in order to understand selling we need to go further than these all too common stereotypes. Because I believe, and so will you by the time you have finished reading this chapter, that selling makes the world go round.

1

According to the song, money makes the world go round. A catchy song, but factually incorrect. It is selling – not money – that makes the world go round.

Nothing Happens Until Someone Sells Something

Pause for a moment while reading this book and take a look around you. Take a good look around the environment you are in. Apart from very few items, everything will have been sold.

As I am writing these words:

I am using my laptop – which was sold to me by a very helpful salesperson at the computer shop.

I am using Microsoft Word   a salesperson from Microsoft will be involved somewhere along the way. Yes, even the mighty Microsoft has sales people!

My laptop is plugged into the mains   I signed up for my current electricity supplier when a salesperson knocked on my front door and told me that I could save money by switching suppliers.

My laptop is sitting on my desk   sold to me by the salesperson at the office suppliers.

I am sitting on my chair also sold to me by the same salesperson at the same office suppliers! A great example of selling, I was buying a desk so they sold me a chair to go with it. And come to think of it, a filing cabinet and a desk lamp too! Now that's what I call selling!

My office is in my house – which was sold to me by an estate agent. I could carry on!

And indeed I shall...

Even if you go to buy a pint of milk from your local shop you can be certain that selling was responsible for it... someone from a wholesaler sold the shop the milk to sell to you... someone sold the shop owner the till to put your money in... someone sold the owner of the shop the fridge your milk is stored in... someone sold the owner the sticky price labels to put on the milk... someone sold the shopkeeper the system he or she uses to organise the wages to pay the person who is taking your money and putting it into the till and so on and so forth.

The very reason that you are reading this book is that I sold the idea to my publisher, Lean Marketing Press, and convinced them to publish it. I had to sell them the concept that it was a good idea for a book. If I had not sold them on the idea, you would not be reading this!

Any company or organisation needs a variety of people so that it can operate effectively. So let's hear it for all the great people from accounts, marketing, warehousing, delivery, customer service, manufacturing, research and development, IT, human resources, training and so on! And if you are a one person business then give yourself a big pat on the back because you deserve it!

However, all of these people rely on the sales people. If the sales people don't sell, then the rest of the company falls over. Everyone, yes everyone, in a company relies upon the sales people.

Nothing happens – no deliveries, no marketing budget, no accounts receivable, no customers to provide service to – until someone sells something.

I want to impress on you how vitally important selling is. Nothing happens until someone sells something. So if you want to make things happen for your company then you need to get good, really damn good, at selling.

Selling Is The Oldest Profession In The World

The entire commercial history of mankind has revolved around selling. Business from its earliest form to today's commercial world has revolved around the essential selling process.

Therefore, if nothing happens until someone sells something, then it has to be the oldest profession in the world! I do appreciate that some of you reading this may consider something else to be the oldest profession in the world. However, that is just a subset of selling, isn't it?

But I'm Not A Salesperson!

You may or may not consider yourself to be a "salesperson". I am guessing the fact that you are reading this book means you have an interest in selling. Perhaps you don't like to consider yourself as a salesperson because of the stereotypes that exist about the selling profession.

However, even if you have never been in a selling role you have still been involved in selling. You see, when you succeeded at getting a job after an interview, you sold yourself. When you convinced someone that you were right about something, that your idea was a good one, you were selling. You may not have thought that you were selling, but that is what you were doing!

I firmly believe that anyone can become good at selling. The Bare Knuckle Selling process will enable you to sell, and sell well.

Why Selling Should Be A Reputable & Honest Profession

Let us leave the stereotypical salesperson concept and really understand what selling is about. There are, and probably always will be, people who manipulate and con people who may be referred to as "sales people". They are not, in my book, sales people.

Sales people, and the process of selling, is the essential process that keeps the modern commercial world turning. Nothing happens until someone sells something!

Selling involves helping people to understand what they need and then, if your product or service can genuinely help them, convincing them to buy it. Please note the "if" in that last sentence. The "if" is very important!

The Bare Knuckle Selling Mirror Test

This test is very simple and very powerful. If you want to be really successful at selling then you need to do it. Go and stand in front of a mirror. Look yourself straight in the eyes and ask yourself if your products and services, and how you sell them, genuinely helps people and adds value to their lives or businesses.

If the answer is a resounding "yes" then you will be able to give yourself fully to selling. If there is any hesitation, then you need to examine what it is you sell and how you sell it.

When you sell properly you don't need to con, manipulate, bamboozle or rip anyone off. You simply make sure you understand what someone really needs and then help them to get it. That is what selling is about. That is something you can be proud of. If the person does not need, and will not benefit from, your product or service then just move onto someone who will. In this way selling just becomes easier and easier, as you build up a larger and larger base of clients and customers who will recommend your products and services to others.

In this way, selling can be regarded as an honest and reputable profession. It is a profession that you can be proud to be a part of.

The 3 Rules of Bare Knuckle Selling

Here are three simple rules. If you follow them then your success in selling is guaranteed.

Rule 1: Your customers (and customers to be) are not stupid.

In today's world people are more educated and informed than ever before. People are more sophisticated and discerning. People just don't fall for blatant and manipulative tactics. I get a little frustrated when I am told that, "the sale ends on Friday". *I* know, and *you* know, that it is immediately replaced with a new sale that starts on Saturday!

People know that there is no such thing as a free lunch. No one is very surprised (or excited) when they get selected to enter the Reader's Digest free prize draw. So, the successful salesperson treats their customers and customers to be with the respect they deserve.

Rule 2: Sell how you like to be sold to.

When I ask people how they like to be sold to, I always get some very similar responses. People like to be treated with respect and courtesy. People like to be listened to. People like the salesperson to be really interested in finding out what they want. People want the salesperson to put *their* interests first. People want to be helped to make a decision that is right for them. Why then would anyone attempt to sell any differently? To a certain extent you already know what good selling is!

Rule 3: Sell only to people who need what you've got.

People are convinced that sales people want to sell them something. They are right, so tell them what 'you're up to'...

Perhaps because of previous encounters, people can be rather suspicious of sales people. In the back of their mind they are worried that the salesperson will try to push them into buying something they don't want. To overcome this fear, just tell people what you are doing.

Tell them that your company exists by engaging in commercial transactions or relationships with customers. You provide products and/or services to customers and they pay money for them. However, what you do first is to understand what is important to the prospective customer. When you understand this, you will see *if* your products and/or services can help them. And, if they can, then you will recommend an appropriate solution. The customer can then decide to say "yes" or "no" to the proposal. By being up front with the customer you remove any fears they may have and establish trust with them.

The Bare Knuckle Selling Process

When people first encounter the concept of a process or a structure for selling, they sometimes worry that this will make them into some sort of selling robot. The Bare Knuckle Selling process does exactly the opposite!

When you have internalised a robust selling process, this allows you to respond instinctively and automatically when you are in front of a customer. The process acts as a guideline or as a handrail to guide you through the sale.

In order to be successful at selling, you must have a structure. If you do not have a robust selling structure then you can lose track of where you are during the sales call. In the to and fro of the conversation with the customer you may drift off track and lose the plot - and the sale. You may forget to cover some important areas which may later jeopardise the sale.

There are no slick sales scripts to follow with Bare Knuckle Selling. There is no "one size fits all" approach with Bare Knuckle Selling. We will be treating all of our customers as unique individuals, with a unique set of needs. We will be treating each and every one of our customers with respect. We will remain flexible and yet disciplined in our approach.

With Bare Knuckle Selling, you will have a robust and reliable process that will guide you through the essential steps of a good sales call. The process is a guide - not a cage. You will be able to be yourself, to use *your* style, *your* personality and *your* words. In this way you will come across as natural and authentic to your customers. You will be able to combine your own unique personal style with a robust and reliable process to guide you through the sales call. This is an unbeatable combination.

The Ten Steps of Bare Knuckle Selling

Here are the ten steps that we will be covering in detail as you read further:

Before the sales call

Step 1: Plan and Prepare

Step 2: Set SMASH objectives and get into a "Top Ten State"

During the sales call

Step 3: Introduce, Hook and get Rapport

Step 4: Understand customer needs and criteria

Step 5: Understand the customer's budget

Step 6: Get the agreement to proceed

Step 7: Propose and Present

Step 8: Reinforce needs, criteria and solutions

Step 9: Secure the result

After the sales call

Step 10: Follow Up

When followed correctly, these ten steps will take you to new heights of selling success.

Please note that throughout the book I will be referring to the people you are selling to as customers. I appreciate that some of the people you will be selling to will be prospective customers (or prospects as they are known in the selling profession) but for ease I have referred to all of these people as customers. Who knows, perhaps if you act as if all of your prospects already are customers then more of them will be!

So without any delay, please join me in the next chapter where we will look at the first step of the Bare Knuckle Selling process...

The 2P Principle

This stage in the Bare Knuckle Selling process, if mastered, will immediately catapult you to the top 10% of the selling profession. This is the step that is often overlooked by many sales "professionals". I would be so bold as to suggest that if they are overlooking this step then they are not all that professional anyway.

Step 1 of the Bare Knuckle Selling process: "Plan and Prepare"

I am sure that you have been told about the importance of planning and preparing before. You will probably have heard the saying: "If you fail to plan you plan to fail."

I have a saying that I use when running seminars on selling. It is: "I know you *know it,* but do you *do it?*" I know full well that some of the things I will mention people will have heard of before. I also know that you already know about the importance of planning and preparation. If you were in the Boy Scouts you will have been told to "Be prepared." Due to my gender I'm not sure what they told the Girl Guides, but I'm willing to guess it was something similar!

Many of the things I suggest people do if they want to be more successful at selling are common sense. However what is common *sense* is not always common *practice.*

That's why I say to people on my seminars, "I know you know it. That's not really that important. What is really important is   *do you do it?*"

By the time you have finished reading this chapter, you will fully understand why you must do your planning and preparation every single time! It really can make the difference between success and failure.

A common objection (or rather excuse) that I am given is that people don't have enough time to prepare. People will tell me that they don't have the time to plan and prepare their sales calls. They just need to get on and do them.

It would appear however, that they do have the time to waste on making sales calls that are unproductive and unsuccessful. Calls that are not planned and prepared are far less likely to be successful. You can also waste a potential customer's time as well as your own. Hardly a tactic that will build a strong commercial relationship is it?

To illustrate the value of investing time (and I do see it as an investment that delivers a return) into planning and preparation, allow me to tell a personal story.

Many years ago I was working as the sales manager of a telephone selling department. Although I was the manager, the company was relatively small and the pay was not too wonderful. I had taken the job initially to get selling experience as I wanted to develop a career in sales. But now it was time for a change.

I applied for a sales job with a major blue chip company. I knew that this company had an enviable reputation for the quality of its sales people. I was determined to secure a sales position as I knew I would get some of the very best sales training available in the country and possibly even the world.

I succeeded in getting an initial interview and knew that I had to make a good impression if I wanted to go to the next stage   an assessment centre.

I knew that I had to plan and be prepared.

So, after work one evening, I went to my local business library. I spent several hours researching and reading up on the company I wanted to work for. I photocopied pages and pages of information on the company and took them home. At home I spent several hours reading through the information and capturing the key points.

I then typed these up into a small dossier on the company. By the time I had finished I knew who the directors were, the history of the company, the brands and products they sold, their key locations around the world and so on.

I then paid a visit to local companies that used their products. I explained that I was going for a job interview, and would they tell me about the company's products, and what they thought about them from a customer's point of view. I collated their feedback and comments and added them to my dossier.

On the day of the initial interview I was faced with a very tough looking sales director. He was conducting a very demanding interview and was really putting me through the mill!

After about ten minutes he asked me what I knew about the company. This was my big moment! For the following five minutes I told him everything I knew about the organisation. His face, that was up until this stage fierce and frowning, started to look somewhat amazed. He interrupted my flow of information and said, "You seem to know a lot about our company!"

I opened my briefcase and took out my dossier and all of the photocopies I had made. I said, "I have spent many hours researching your company. I am very serious about wanting to work for you. Would you like to know what your customers think of your products and your current sales people?"

He stared at me open mouthed for a moment, and then indicated that indeed he was interested in hearing what his customers thought.

At the end of the interview he said, "You will definitely be hearing from us!" And I did. I succeeded in passing the assessment centre and was offered a job. The job immediately doubled my current salary. I also got a brand new company car, which meant that I could sell my current car and bank the money.

I calculated that each hour of time I had spent in research and preparation was worth over £1000 to me in financial gain in the first year alone. I also benefited from an in depth induction into the company which included a four week residential sales training programme.

Four weeks sales training from one of the most professional and highly regarded companies in the country!

I cannot begin to calculate what the training alone has been worth to me in salary, commissions and bonuses over the years. Those hours of planning and preparation have made a massive contribution to my finances!

You can't always predict what life long value a customer will bring to you in terms of business and profit. You can't always predict how many other potential customers a customer will introduce you to. It pays to plan. It pays to prepare.

How To Plan

Know who is buying your (or similar) products and services

You need to identify the market sectors of current buyers of your product or service. Learn about the industries of these customers. What kind of customers are buying? Who might be buying in the future?

If you specialise in a particular market, industry or sector then you need to understand it! You need to understand who *is* buying and who *might* be buying so that you can target them. You must identify your 'best fit' customer market and concentrate on it.

Know who the big fish are

It is important to plan who to target. Many sales people are put off targeting large companies and wealthy individuals. They assume that these organisations and individuals will already be well targeted by other sales people. Sometimes, nothing is further from the truth! In the same way that some supermodels never get approached by men because everyone assumes they can pick and choose, large companies and wealthy people are often under prospected. Rich, powerful people are still just people. Don't assume that the biggest prospects are already taken.

If you sell executive coaching services, you would find it more lucrative to work with an organisation with an executive coaching budget of £200k (which is not uncommon), rather than targeting a smaller company with a £5k budget.

As the famous speaker and writer Brian Tracy says, "If you go fishing for minnows you need a thousand of them to fill a bucket. If you go fishing for whales and you catch one, it fills the boat."

There is a principle known as the Pareto Principle. It is named after an Italian economist called Vilfredo Pareto who observed that 80% of the wealth in Italy was in the hands of 20% of the population. Although the exact percentages may vary, this principle seems to apply, almost uncannily, to many areas of life. 80% of your profits will come from 20% of your products, 80% of your turnover will come from 20% of your customers and so on.

It is not that smaller customers are not important. It is a very good thing to have a balanced customer portfolio, and not to become over reliant on a small group of customers. However the potential rewards from bigger and wealthier customers can be so much greater. Or to re word the famous line from George Orwell's book 'Animal Farm', "All customers are equal, but some are more equal than others."

Know your customer's businesses

In the same way that I researched the company I wanted to work for, you need to research the companies that you want as customers. The level of detail will depend upon the level of contact and the potential size or value of the customer to you. It would not be practical to spend hours researching a long list of companies that you are making an initial cold call to. However, it is necessary if you want to secure significant business from a large company or organisation.

If you are going fishing for whales then you must do your research. For many organisations you can find out a lot about them before you have any contact with them. Potential sources of data include anyone who has contact or involvement with them, their competitors, sales people from other companies who may deal with them, the internet, the national, local or trade press, Yellow Pages, directories from your local business library (including Kompass, Kelly's, Dun & Bradstreet), lists of members from trade associations, recruitment advertisements in the press and catalogues from trade fairs or exhibitions.

Some of the information you may wish to keep in your customer profile includes:

- Name of company and subsidiaries, addresses of offices, factories, shops, outlets. Telephone numbers, fax numbers, mobile numbers, website details etc.
- Financial information such as turnover, shareholders etc.
- Key personnel such as board of directors, senior management, buyers etc.
- Management or organisational structure.
- Number of employees.
- Details of their brands, products and services.
- Major competitors.
- Current suppliers.
- Press cuttings featuring the customer.

Devise a format (paper based or electronic customer record card) for storing this information that works for you and keep it updated. All professional sales people keep up to date information on their prospects and customers in this way.

Information on the individual prospect/customer contact

Professional sales people also keep up to date information on the individuals that they do business with or aim to do business with. As well as the more obvious things like name (with phonetic spelling also to ensure correct pronunciation), address, direct telephone number, fax number, email address and mobile phone   you may like to add other personal information.

This can include partner's names, children's names, birthdays, hobbies outside of work, areas of personal interest both inside and outside of work, membership of professional and business associations, favourite sports, favourite football teams, favourite food and so on. It is also a good idea to know their secretary or PA's name. Saying, "Hello, is that Chris?" when the secretary answers your phone call builds rapport. It pays to have a good relationship with someone's secretary or PA! Far too may sales people under estimate the amount of influence these people have and how much they can help or hinder your success depending upon your relationship with them.

Obviously, if you are selling direct to members of the public and not organisations, then the type and amount of information you are going to be able to collect and use will be less detailed.

However, you must keep organised and up to date information on each and every customer.

Read in your chosen field

It is important to keep up to date in your chosen industry or field. Professional sales people make a point of regular reading in their chosen field or in the industry sector of the customers they have selected to target.

If you are selling financial services then you will need to read the relevant trade magazines and press in this area on a regular and on going basis. If you are selling financial services to the motor industry then you would also want to add relevant motor industry magazines and journals to your regular reading.

Many industries or publications that cover these industries have email newsletters to which you can subscribe to. This makes it very easy to keep up to speed.

It is not difficult to keep up to date in any area. The ability to knowledgably discuss the latest news or trends with your prospects and customers makes you look like the selling professional that you are.

What To Prepare

My own personal rule is to prepare anything that I may need when I am face to face with the customer. It is very professional to be able to answer any question your prospect or customer may have on the spot. This communicates a professional and business like message to your customers.

Some suggestions for things to prepare are:

- Know your products and services in detail.
- Know your competitor's products and services in detail.
- Know your prices
- Know your competitor's prices
- Have a range of sales aids to help your sales presentation – these could include brochures, press clippings, samples, testimonials from existing customers etc.
- Have a simple presentation on your product and service in a presentation folder or on your laptop.
- If you need to use your laptop in a sales call make sure it is clean and the battery is fully charged. Take your power cable also, as you can plug it in if the customer is happy with you doing this.
- If you need to present to more than one person in a call, either take multiple copies of your presentation or take a data projector with you.
- Make sure your mobile 'phone is fully charged each day.

- Make sure you have directions or a map to your customer's offices/home.

- Have a smart briefcase or bag that contains all you may need including pens, pencils, notepad, business cards, diary and organiser.

It is very important that you practice any sales presentation that you may make to a prospect or customer. As you will discover later you will not be making scripted presentations, but you must know the elements of your presentation inside out so that you can flex and adapt it to suit each individual. Practice, practice, practice.

Finally, make sure you prepare yourself personally. Make sure your appearance is appropriate. You may choose to wear a suit if that is appropriate. Sometimes I wear a suit, sometimes I do not. If I am calling on a customer who is very casual I will take a different approach. I once looked after a very large customer who dressed informally in the office. It was not unusual to see the Managing Director walking around the office in a t shirt, trainers and tracksuit bottoms. And that was when he was dressing smartly! So I followed his lead and would often turn up in an open necked shirt and trousers, which helped me to be seen more like him than the other sales people who looked over dressed in their suits and ties.

Although society is gradually becoming more liberated, people are still judged on how they look. If you have an unusual hairstyle, facial piercing, pierced ears if you are a man, tattoos, a moustache or beard (particularly striking if you are female!), unusual clothes and so on, then people will make judgements about you. I'm not saying this is right, I am just telling you how it is. It is your choice about how appropriate your appearance is in relation to the prospects and customers you are targeting. Just be aware that people make very fast judgements based upon appearance. Get your appearance wrong and you could lose sales before you even get started.

Please don't smoke or drink alcohol before meeting prospects and customers. More and more people are now non smokers and find the smell off putting. If you do smoke then do it well before seeing a prospect or customer and take some mints or mouthwash with you.

By getting your planning and preparation done thoroughly, you are maximising your chances of being in front of the very best customers and prospects with all the ammunition you need to sign up some profitable business. Get this wrong and the more professional sales people will run rings around you!

As a Bare Knuckle Seller it should be your competitors who are feeling the pain – not you!

SMASH Your Way To Success

In this chapter we are going to look at the vitally important area of setting very specific objectives for your sales calls. Far too many sales people have a very poor idea of what they want to achieve from each sales call.

Step 2 of the Bare Knuckle Selling process:
"Set SMASH objectives and get into a 'Top Ten State'"

A weak objective (if indeed there is any objective at all) results in weak selling.

Sales people with weak objectives can annoy customers. They are the sales people who pay a visit to a customer to 'maintain the relationship'.

Sales calls like this are sometimes referred to as 'cappuccino calls'. The salesperson and the customer achieve absolutely nothing of value other than having a cup of coffee together.

Please don't misunderstand me, I am not saying that developing and maintaining a good relationship with your customers is not important. It is *very* important. However, I am going to show you ways to do this that are far more effective than simply having coffee together.

Cappuccino calls can also have exactly the opposite effect! You can annoy your customer by wasting his time. He may have lots to do but is just being polite to you. All the way through the coffee and chat he is thinking of all the things he has to do, and he is hoping that you will hurry up and go away so that he can get on with them!

If you want to be one of the very best sales people around and make your competitors quake in their boots at the very mention of your name, then you simply must set powerful selling objectives.

The Power of Setting Goals and Objectives

It is not possible to read any self improvement book or attend any motivation seminar without the subject of goals being mentioned. By the way, my books and seminars are no different!

As I have been a passionate advocate of goal and objective setting for many years, I became interested in understanding what psychological research had been conducted into goal setting, and what proven, scientific conclusions had been reached.

To discover the answer I spent many months wading through huge volumes of psychological research. I have a deep interest in this area (perhaps I need to get out a bit more often) and left no stone unturned.

One of the strongest pieces of research I discovered was a review of well over one hundred psychological studies on goal setting. It concluded that, "the beneficial effect of goal setting on task performance is one of the most robust and replicable findings in psychological literature. Furthermore, these effects are found just as reliable in field settings as in the laboratory."

In layman's language this means that if you want to improve your performance then you must set goals. Goals set out specific standards that will motivate you to take direct action by focusing attention, increasing effort and intensity, prompting the development of new problem solving strategies and encouraging persistence in the face of failure. This is a proven, scientific fact.

If you want to improve your selling then you must set strong selling objectives. So let's find out exactly how to do this.

S.M.A.S.H. Your Selling Objectives!

The process that follows is strongly recommended when setting your selling objective.

The mnemonic S.M.A.S.H. stands for:

SPECIFIC - MEASURABLE - ACHIEVEABLE - STRETCHING   HOLISTIC

SPECIFIC

It is important to know specifically what it is that you want. Your selling objective must be stated in the positive: What you *do* want rather than what you *do not* want.

Research demonstrates that explicit, specific and numerical (where appropriate) objectives are more effective in facilitating behavioural change. If you want to see improvements in your selling ability, then you must set specific and measurable goals.

You do not go shopping in a supermarket by making a list of all the things you don't want. You make a list of the things you *do* want to get. Do the same when setting your selling objectives. It is understood that the unconscious mind (everything you are not thinking about with your conscious mind at this moment) cannot process negative commands. In order to think of something you do not want, you have to think and focus your attention upon that very thing.

It is also theorised that the information flows into the unconscious mind almost instantly, whereas the conscious mind will take a few seconds longer to process something. So by the time your conscious mind has processed your goal to stop doing something (e.g. smoking) your unconscious mind has already processed the concept of smoking in order to make sense of the goal. Your unconscious mind is now focused on the very thing you consciously want to stop doing!

The 'specific' step defines the result you want in a clear and unambiguous way.

MEASURABLE

How will you know when you have achieved your goal? What will it look, sound and feel (taste and smell) like?

If, for example, you set a selling objective to "get more sales" and someone gave you a very small order would you have achieved your goal? You wouldn't know! Exactly how much "more sales" is meant by "get more sales"?

Create a sensory rich, specific goal. The more sensory specific data you can include, the more your brain has to lock onto.

It is also important to set specific dates by which you will achieve your sales objectives. These dates will provide a reminder and create a sense of positive urgency.

The 'measured' step provides clear success criteria.

ACHIEVEABLE

Is the achievement of your selling objective realistic for your circumstances and those of your customer or prospect?

Firstly, if you are selling computers to a small business owner who has an annual turnover of £50,000 per year, it is rather unlikely that he will be prepared to spend £100,000 on a new networked computer system.

Secondly, are you capable of delivering the products or services that you are selling?

Providing a network of trainers around the world to meet the needs of a multi national corporation might be a tad challenging if you have a staff of just you and your Mum who helps out with the typing every Friday.

The 'achievable' step provides "can do" motivation.

STRETCHING

Is your selling objective challenging enough?

Research demonstrates that specific and challenging goals lead to a higher level of performance than easy goals.

There is a direct relationship between goal difficulty and task performance. The more difficult a goal, the better the performance.

While care should be taken to ensure that your selling objectives are challenging though not unrealistic, laboratory based studies have shown positive relationships between goal difficulty and performance, even in the case of unattainable goals!

The 'stretching' step provides the inspiration to become bolder and more ambitious in your selling.

HOLISTIC

Will the achievement of your selling objective be good for your customer and for you?

It is very important that your selling objective has considered the potential needs of the customer as well as the benefit to you. Far too may sales people have only got their own commission in mind when selling.

If the achievement of your selling objective will benefit the customer then you stand the greatest chance of achieving it. It needs to be holistic for both parties concerned.

The 'holistic' step provides a good win/win outcome for your selling efforts.

The Power of Writing Down Your Objectives

I had the privilege of meeting Tony Buzan recently. Tony is the creator of the Mind Mapping concept and an expert in the ability of the human brain. Tony told me that he has been reviewing research that concludes that the mere act of writing your objectives down increases your likelihood of achieving them by 25%!

So always, always, always write your selling objectives down.

Here is the SMASH objective that I wrote down before approaching Lean Marketing Press with the idea for my book:

SPECIFIC

Lean Marketing Press will accept my book "Bare Knuckle Selling" for publication.

MEASUREABLE

A signed contract by 30th February 2005.

ACHIEVEABLE

Yes. I can write the book, Lean Marketing Press can publish the book.

STRETCHING

I have sold many things but never an idea for a book before!

HOLISTIC

Lean Marketing Press secure a good book for their 'selling' list which will enhance their portfolio. I get publicity and author's royalties. Win Win!

Once you have completed your planning and preparation and written down your SMASH objective, you will be almost ready to make you sales call. There is however, one very important thing you need to do just before you call on the customer.

The Inner Game: Your 'Top Ten State'

When top sports people prepare for competitions they warm up physically. They do this to ensure that their muscles and joints are ready to compete at the highest level. What is becoming more and more common is for these athletes to also warm up mentally.

Almost every single elite athlete will now have a sports psychologist who will train them how to mentally prepare to win.

As someone who wants to become one of the selling elite, you will also benefit from a mental warm up prior to making your sales calls.

Are You In a Bit of a State?

Have you ever had the misfortune of meeting someone who has 'got out of bed on the wrong side'? Perhaps you have even experienced this sort of feeling yourself!

When people are emotionally and/or physically at a low ebb, we may describe them as being in 'a bit of a state'. We also know that in order to perform, or even to begin certain tasks successfully, we need to be in 'the right state of mind'.

So let us define 'state'. State can be described as the total ongoing mental and physical conditions from which a person is acting. It is a combination of all of the thoughts, emotions and physiology that are expressed at any given moment – our mental pictures, feelings, sounds, physical energy, posture and breathing.

Your state changes on an on going basis. Some states feel better than others and some are better states to be in if you wish to perform certain tasks successfully. Generalised states that might enable you to sell effectively could include 'confident', 'happy', 'calm' or 'powerful'. Generalised states that may not be so helpful could include 'confused', 'fearful', 'anxious' or 'frustrated'.

Psyching Up and Psyching Down

Athletes are trained by sports psychologists to get themselves into an appropriate state of activation (readiness to perform) for the specific events in which they are competing. They may 'psych up' or 'psych down' as appropriate.

Your performance is affected by the state you are in. Have you ever tried to perform a delicate and complex task when feeling angry? It be useful to be able to exercise some choice over the states you experience wouldn't it?

What Is State Management?

State Management is the ability to choose the most appropriate state at any given moment. State Management gives you the choice about the state you want to be in.

In order to perform to the best of your ability, the facility to choose and manage your own state, to be in the optimal mental, emotional and physical state for the specific task at hand is a useful skill.

By using a series of specific techniques you can alter your state at will, maintain positive states for longer periods and change negative states into more empowering ones. You will take control. When you are in an appropriate and resourceful state, your selling performance can improve.

What Creates The State We're In?

There are two main components that affect and (are affected by) our state:

1) Your internal representations

2) Your physiology

Internal Representations

What you picture and how you picture things inside your mind, plus what you say to yourself and how you say it contribute towards the state you are in. How you perceive and represent the world to yourself powerfully affects your state. Your beliefs, values, attitudes and past experiences all affect the kinds of internal representations you make.

Physiology

In terms of our physiology, factors such as what we eat, drink and how tired we are will all have an influence on our state. What is less well recognised is that other physiological factors can also affect your state positively or negatively.

These include how you are breathing, your levels of muscular tension and your posture.

The Body Mind System

What is not always fully appreciated is that the body and the mind are not two separate parts or divisions. They are one unified system. The body affects the mind and the mind affects the body.

In order to demonstrate this, I would like to invite you to take part in an exercise. Vividly imagine the following scene as it is described...

Imagine that you are sitting at a table. On the table in front of you is a bowl of crushed ice. Sitting on top of the crushed ice is a very large and very juicy lemon that has been cut into quarters. Pick up one of the quarters of lemon. Notice how when you squeeze it, drops of lemon juice ooze out of it. Lift up the quarter of lemon to your nose and smell the sharp scent of the lemon. Now place the quarter of lemon into your mouth and bite it, feeling the lemon juice burst all over your tongue!

If you have imagined this scene vividly you will find that you mouth is now full of saliva! Merely biting the lemon in your imagination has resulted in a physical response from your body. What you have imagined in your mind has affected your body.

In a similar way, we will all have experienced our body affecting our mind. Feeling physically tired, for example, can affect how we are thinking and feeling. If we are experiencing any form of physical pain from an injury or illness, this may also affect how we are feeling mentally. Conversely, feeling well rested and healthy can help us to experience a more positive and happy state of mind.

Although we will all be able to identify with these influences, what is not always appreciated is that we can consciously use our physiology to change our state. It is literally possible to *choose and change your state.*

How to Use Your Physiology To Change Your State

To demonstrate how physiology affects our state, imagine for a moment that you are feeling very negative and unhappy. Now move your body into the sort of posture it would be in if you felt like this. How would you sit or stand if you were feeling like this? Would you be slumped in your chair? How would your face look? Would you be frowning? How would your breathing be if you were feeling negative? Would it be low and shallow? There will be a specific physiology that goes along with these negative thoughts.

Now let us change our state! Sit or stand in the posture you would be in if you were feeling very positive, confident and happy! How would you be sitting or standing? Would you be upright with your shoulders back? How would your face look? Would you have a big smile on your face? How would you be breathing? Would it be deep and full? Again, there will be a specific physiology that goes along with these positive thoughts.

You will find it almost impossible to feel negative if you have a positive body posture. One way to change how you are feeling, very quickly, is to change your physiology.

If you want to feel more positive, upbeat and confident sit, stand and move like you are feeling positive, upbeat and confident. Because the body and mind are one unified system, your physiology will affect your mind and change the state you are in.

This powerful technique is deceptively simple. Please experiment with it and notice how you can change your state at will.

Mental Rehearsal

Mental rehearsal is the process of practicing mentally. For example, you could imagine in your mind the selling process you will go through with your customer with all the various directions it may take. You could imagine potential sticking points ahead of time and rehearse ways in which you'd be able to keep the meeting on track and emerge with a new contract. Although this sounds very simple, mental rehearsal is a very powerful method of performance enhancement.

There is a famous story about an American army officer who was held captive for several years during the Vietnam war. In order to keep himself occupied he would play a game of golf in his imagination every day. When he was finally released from captivity, he went to play an actual game of golf for the first time in many years. He played one of the best games of golf in his life the many years of *mental* rehearsal had resulted in a huge improvement in his *physical* golfing performance!

Almost 100% of Olympic athletes surveyed by sports psychologist reported the use of mental rehearsal. Elite athletes use this technique for one reason and one reason only – it works. Mental rehearsal is a powerful performance enhancement method.

How To Talk To Yourself!

Relax there is no need to be alarmed! Talking to yourself, despite common misconceptions, is not a sign of mental illness!

Talking to yourself, or 'Self Talk' as it is referred to by sports psychologists, is a powerful method of controlling your thinking and therefore your performance.

You are engaging in self talk any time you carry on dialogue with yourself. This could be giving yourself instructions and encouragement, or interpreting what you are feeling about a situation. This dialogue can occur out loud or inside your head.

Self talk is a powerful technique of mental control and as such can be an asset when it enhances feelings of self worth and performance.

However, it can equally be a dangerous liability when it is negative, or if it distracts you from the task you are engaged in. In my experience, many people will say derogatory things about themselves, or to themselves, that they would never dream about saying to another person.

According to research, the average person in Britain will use *fourteen* times more negative references than positive references when talking about themselves and the job that they do. I consider this to be a concerning statistic.

The use of negative self talk affects not only performance. It can affect people's overall self esteem. In extreme cases this could lead to depression. Certain forms of depression have been described as nothing more than a disorder of conscious thought, and not a matter of brain chemistry or anger turned inwards, as other theories maintain. Some depressed people simply think awful things about themselves and their future. Their symptom, negative self talk, is their dis ease!

Researchers have found that good self talk can produce significant changes in performance. For example, it has been found that runners who say words to themselves such as 'quick' or 'fast' do indeed increase their running speed!

So how does this work? We have already explored that the mind and the body are not separate, but two aspects of an integrated system. The mind affects the body and the body affects the mind. What appears to happen is that the act of repeating a negative word causes the body to respond in a negative (or weaker) manner, and the repeating of a positive word causes the body to respond in a positive (or stronger) manner.

The Triple Grand Slam!

By combining state management, mental rehearsal and self talk together you can prepare yourself to maximise your chances of selling success.

When you meet the customer you will be feeling calm, relaxed, confident and assured of success. This will make a powerful impact on the customer not only when they first meet you but also during the entire sales process.

This process can be completed in a matter of a few minutes before you go to meet your customer. Much of it can be done as you walk from you car to the customer's offices for example. The process to follow is:

1. Mentally rehearse a highly successful sales call

2. See yourself having achieved your SMASH objective

3. Make your posture powerful and upright. Walk and move like you do when you feel calm, powerful and confident.

4. Breathe as you would when you feel calm, powerful and confident.

5. Say to yourself, "I'm the best", "I am superb at selling", "I am the greatest salesperson ever". Say it with passion and feeling.

6. Meet your customer and achieve your SMASH objective!

As the cliché goes, "You never get a second chance to make a first impression." A salesperson who has done their planning and preparation, has set a strong SMASH objective, who has mentally rehearsed and who has said positive things to themselves is going to make a strong impression as a calm, relaxed professional who is here to do business. Your customers will respond very positively when you make that sort of an impression! And we haven't even started to talk to them yet!

Get Hooking!

So after having planned and prepared thoroughly, set a robust SMASH objective and got ourselves into a winning state through using mental preparation, all we have to do is to sell our product or service to the customer!

Step 3 of the Bare Knuckle Selling process: "Introduce, Hook and get Rapport"

In order to achieve a successful sale it is vital that you make a powerful first impression, introduce yourself, grab your prospect or customer's attention and develop rapport with them.

So let's take these one at a time in a nice and easy step by step process!

First Impression

Having heeded the comments in the first chapter regarding appearance (and having removed your silver nose bone piercing before going to see your customer), making a good first impression is actually very simple.

When you meet your customer, make good eye contact, offer a firm handshake and SMILE! As simple as these three things are, so many people mess them up.

Making eye contact sends a message of confidence to the customer. People who don't make good eye contact are sometimes regarded as being somehow shifty or untrustworthy. Not an ideal association for a salesperson to have.

A firm handshake, whether you are male or female is important. People make conscious and unconscious judgement about people from their handshake.

A limp, 'wet fish' style handshake (YUK!) can be very off putting! At the other extreme some people have a real 'bone crusher' of a handshake that apart from being potentially painful is also off putting. Some people think that having a very powerful handshake exudes power and can intimidate people into a more submissive role in the subsequent meeting. However, an attempt by someone to crush every bone in your hand can be an indication of insecurity. I prefer to exude calm confidence which I believe is more professional and effective.

If you have any concerns about your handshake, find a trusted friend and do some practice!

Smile! Smile! Smile! Nothing is better for creating a positive first impression than a smile. A smile is welcoming and appealing. When first meeting a customer, having a face like a smacked backside is hardly going to endear you to them is it?

Have some fun in front of your bathroom mirror making sure you have perfected your sincere and genuine smile!

The Great Dane principle

I learned a valuable lesson about selling from a dog I used to own. Ben was a Great Dane. As he was a very large animal he could get interesting responses from people. Although he was a big softy and wouldn't harm a flea, he could do a very effective impression of being a big, fierce guard dog. As Ben weighed well over 150 pounds it really was a very believable act.

Ben's fierce scary dog act was very useful for discouraging unwanted callers such as religious fanatics and somewhat dubious people offering to tarmac my front drive for a bargain price!

When people came to our front door Ben would start his 'I'm a very fierce guard dog' routine. It was interesting to note that Ben's behaviour would be heavily influenced by the reaction of the person.

If they started to look nervous and panic, Ben would escalate 'fierce guard dog' to a full blown snarling 'Hound of the Baskervilles' routine. This would sometimes result in an urgent requirement for a change of underwear for the person on the receiving end!

On the other hand if the person responded with confidence then 'fierce guard dog' would be rapidly scaled down to 'great big softy' which was Ben's true personality.

So depending on how people responded to Ben they would either be pursued down my drive by a homicidal canine or be licked and slobbered on by their new best friend.

In the same way, if you behave in a cheerful, courteous, confident and professional manner towards your prospects and customers, then you are likely to get the same behaviour returned.

If you do ever have the misfortune to be faced with a customer who appears to be big and scary, think of the Great Dane rule – they might just be a big softy underneath!

Introducing Yourself

As basic as introducing yourself to someone is, this is something that many people get wrong. Firstly you need to make sure you are actually talking to the right person. The person who you first see may be an assistant, secretary or colleague.

So, make eye contact, smile, hold out your hand and "Mrs Welch?" or "Sarah?"

It is far safer (and usually far more amusing for the person concerned) to make the mistake of assuming that a secretary is the Managing Director than making the mistake of assuming that the Managing Director is the secretary!

Only use first names if you are confident that it is okay to do so. Depending upon the company and/or the individual the more formal surname may be appropriate.

In a recent survey, 67% of male buyers and 83% of female buyers were okay about being addressed by their first name. That does still leave 33% of men and 17% of women who prefer to be called Mr / Mrs / Miss or Ms. so it's safer not to make assumptions!

Calling a man "Mr." is usually a safe bet. Calling a single woman "Mrs" is not. Some women dislike being addressed as "Miss", preferring "Ms" which is often the safer option. When conducting your initial research, or when booking your appointment, find out which people prefer and then stick to it!

Then (still smiling and making eye contact) "Good morning (unless it's afternoon) Mr Fisher, Simon Hazeldine from E3 Group. Nice to meet you." Make sure you clearly state your name and the company you are from. Although in many instances they will know who you are and where you are from, this avoids any misunderstanding.

If your appointment is pre arranged there may now be some polite small talk about the weather, your journey to see them and so on. This may take place, for example, as you walk together to their office.

Take Control

Do not try to sell anything when you are standing in the foyer or standing in a corridor. In these circumstances it is very difficult for you to get the full attention of the customer and very easy for them to get rid of you!

Be polite and firm: "Is there somewhere quiet we can go where we won't be disturbed?" Be assertive and do your very best to get the customer into their office or somewhere suitable for your sales call. Be prepared to use your hook (dealt with next) to grab their attention.

Hook

The aim of the hook is to grab their attention and get them focusing on you. Before they met you they may have been on the phone talking to a supplier or a customer of their own. They may have a long and pressing list of things to do. You must grab their attention and focus it on you.

When copywriters are writing direct mail letters they can spend up to 90% of their time writing just the headline at the top of the letter. Good copywriters know that unless they grab your attention with a compelling headline, their direct mail letter will go unread and probably end up in the bin!

It is equally important that you grab the attention of your customers when making a sales call.

Your hook should:

1) Answer the customer's question: "Why should I listen to you?"

2) Cause them to be curious and ask the question: "What is it?"

Questions as Hooks

The use of questions can be very powerful hooks. Questions engage the customer. Asking questions enables you to engage people's brains and draw them into your world!

In addition it is impossible to not answer a question! When you ask someone a question, they have to answer it internally at the very least, even if they don't answer it out loud.

Examples include:

"Would you be interested in a proven method that can increase your sales by 20% in the next 12 months?"

"Would you be interested in saving £1,000 per month on your marketing costs?"

All good hooks will include something that will benefit the customer. They will focus on what is in it for the customer. In this way they will capture attention.

"You Know How..."

The following is a very nice formula that you can use as a hook:

The structure is:

"You know how (problem) which (effect of problem)? Well what I do is (solution to problem) which means that (benefit)."

Example:

"Mr Customer, you know how **tough it can be finding new customers,** which **makes it difficult to grow your business?** Well, what I do is **show business people like you innovative new ways to find new customers,** which means that **future growth and profits are so much easier.**"

You do not have to stick to the exact words but it is important to stick to the overall pattern. Here is another example of how I would use it:

"Mr Customer you know how sometimes your sales people fail to close the sales that they should, and as a result they lose sales to the competition? What I do is to use a totally unique method to train sales people to dramatically improve their ability to close

more sales, which means you can expect to see a sales improvement of between 10 and 20%."

To add additional power to your hook, it is very useful to nod your head as you ask your first question: "Mr Customer you know how sometimes your sales people fail (start nodding) to close the sales that they should?" This is a powerful method of unconscious suggestion, and you will often find the customer will follow your lead and start nodding too.

I'm Not Buying Anything!

At one stage in my sales career I was selling advertising space and I cold called a prospective customer over the phone and secured an appointment. The prospective customer owned a taxi company and when I called on him at his offices he cheerily greeted me with, "I don't know why you've bothered to call, I'm not going to buy anything."

Not a great start to a sales call you may be thinking! This is however not an entirely unexpected response from many prospective customers. I used an extension to my hook as follows:

"Mr Jones, I'm not going to try to sell anything to you right now. All I'd like to do while I'm here is to show you some of the reasons that other taxi companies are working with us and are benefiting from increased business as a result. All I ask is that you look at what I'm going to show you openly and honestly and decide if it applies to your business, and tell me at the end of this discussion if this is right for you. That's fair, isn't it?"

I nodded as I said, "That's fair, isn't it?" and Mr Jones nodded in return. He invited me into his office. Half an hour later he signed the order, wrote me a cheque and thanked me for taking the time and trouble to come and see him!

If I had not had my hook pre prepared I may never have even got into his office.

Do The Opposite Of What The Customer Expects

Another method that you can use if you experience initial resistance is to do exactly the opposite of what the customer expects.

Some of the early resistance people demonstrate is borne out of a concern about or mistrust of sales people. And with the poor quality and manipulative behaviour of many sales people around today, who can blame them!

For example, a customer might say to you, "Why should I buy from you?" You can do the opposite of what the prospect expects and say "Maybe you shouldn't." This usually provokes a stunned silence!

You can then continue, "Mr Customer, until I understand your business in more detail and identify some of your challenges that I can help you with, I wouldn't even dream of telling you to buy our product. What I'd like to do is to listen to what you have to say and then if there are some areas that I can help you with then we can talk about them then. That's fair, isn't it?"

This is a powerful way of building credibility. Here is a salesperson what wants to listen to what the customer wants to say – what a refreshing change!

I arranged the current mortgage on my house with a salesperson who refused to sell me a mortgage! My wife and I had a fixed rate mortgage with a well known building society. The fixed term was for five years and for the first four years or so it was a fantastic deal. As the final year began the interest rate dropped and the fixed rate we were enjoying was not as competitive.

We contacted the building society who informed us that they would be very happy to re arrange the mortgage and put us onto a different fixed rate mortgage. However, if we decided to move our mortgage to another building society, then we would need to pay a penalty for not completing the full five years of the agreement. We decided to get some independent advice.

One of our friends recommended that we speak to a guy called Martin. Martin does not fit the stereotypical slick salesman. He is a fifty year old, rather shy and retiring gentleman. Martin spent about an hour asking us lots of questions so that he could fully understand our circumstances. Interestingly, the question session was a lot longer and more in depth than with our current building society.

After doing some calculations, Martin said that he didn't think we should change our mortgage. He advised us to stay with our current building society and finish the agreed five year term. We obviously looked slightly confused as this meant paying more money per month for the rest of the year than we needed to.

Martin went on to explain that he had calculated how much we would have saved over the entire five year period. Yes, we were paying a little over the odds now but when this was viewed from the perspective of the whole five years we were well ahead.

In addition, completing the five year period would leave us free of any tie and we could arrange a new mortgage with anyone we chose to. Our existing building society would be happy to re tie us to a new mortgage, but Martin said that he could get far better deals than that once we were free of tie.

After he explained it, the obvious choice was to do as he suggested. Six months later we went back to see Martin and he arranged a brand new mortgage. It was a significantly better deal than we would have got had we pursued our original plans.

It could be said that Martin took a risk in that he may never have seen us again. He could have tried to sell us a new mortgage on the spot but instead he did what was best for us. As a result he got our business and earned our respect.

It is interesting to note that he was recommended to us and we in turn have recommended him to others. We trust Martin, and we do so primarily because of the time when he told us that the best thing for us was not to do anything! He did the opposite of what we expected and he has reaped the rewards.

Gaining Rapport

A vitally important part of any sales call is establishing rapport with your customer. This can be accomplished very easily!

Researchers at Boston University Medical School studied films of people having conversations. The researchers observed that as people were talking they began to unconsciously co ordinate their movements and postures. This is sometimes referred to as 'postural echoing' or 'mirroring'.

When the brainwave activity of these same people was monitored using electroencepholographs, it was found that some of their brain waves were 'spiking' at the same moment.

As the conversations were progressing, people were getting into deeper rapport with each other and their physiology (and body language) was representing this. We have all had the experience of being in rapport with someone. The question is how can we do this deliberately rather than leaving it to chance?

Rapport is commonly known as a sense of ease and connection that develops when you are communicating and interacting with someone you like, trust or feel comfortable with.

An error that some people make when they are first introduced to methods to build rapport is they think they can use them to 'make someone like them' or 'cause people to get rapport with me' or in some way 'do' rapport on someone.

Rapport is a property that emerges out of an interaction between people. It is, if you like, an emergent property of the system that is made up of the people involved.

In this way I do not see rapport methods as being manipulative. I believe they are respectful and help support you in correctly identifying what someone needs and understanding what is important to them.

There are a number of things that you can do to enhance the likelihood of establishing rapport with another person. On a basic level 'people who are like each other tend to like each other'. That is, we like people who are like us.

By observing your customers carefully you can mirror the behaviours of another person and become more 'like' them. To mirror another person, select the behaviour or quality you wish to mirror and then carry out that behaviour. Examples of things that you can mirror are:

PHYSICAL

- Body posture
- Hand gestures
- Tilt of the head
- Facial expression
- Rate of blinking
- Breathing rate

VOCAL

- Pace, rhythm, tonality of their voice
- Key phrases that the person habitually uses

Preferred Representational System

There are many factors that can influence the words that a person uses. One of the most significant factors relates to which of their five senses (sight, sound, touch, taste and smell) they are the most aware of at any given time.

The field of psychology known as Neuro Linguistic Programming (NLP) has revealed that the way that someone is thinking is revealed in their language. People think by using internal representations of their five senses. In NLP these are referred to as representational systems.

If a person is mainly thinking in sounds you may hear phrases such as, *"sounds good to me."*, *"I hear what you are saying."* If a person is mainly thinking in pictures you may hear phrases such as, *"I see what you mean."*, *"Look at it this way."* If a person is thinking mainly in feelings you may hear phrases such as, *"That feels right."*, *"I'd like to get to grips with that."*

Although taste and smell may also be referenced it is usually sight, sound and touch that are the ones that are most often used.

These representational systems are referred to in NLP as visual (seeing), auditory (hearing), kinaesthetic (feeling), olfactory (smelling) and gustatory (tasting). Examples of words associated with each representational system are:

VISUAL

Look, see, picture, imagine, visualise, focus, clear, brilliant, bright, dim etc.

For example: "I like the look of that" or "I see what you mean"

AUDITORY

Hear, listen, sound, ring, buzz, call, echo, harsh, loud, quiet, tell etc.

For example: "I like the sound of that" or "That rings a bell"

KINAESTHETIC

Feel, hold, grip, grab, push, touch, heavy, firm, grapple, pull, warm, cold etc.

For example: "That feels good" or "Let's touch base"

OLFACTORY

Smell, rotten, fishy, fragrance, scent etc.

For example: "The sweet smell of success" or "There's something fishy about this"

GUSTATORY

Taste, bitter, sweet, sharp, salty, bland etc.

For example: "That's a sweet deal" or "It left a bitter taste in my mouth"

While no one uses only one sensory system in all their language, people will tend to have a preference in a given context. Indeed some people have a preference for one main representational system across many contexts!

Speaking to someone using the language from their preferred representational system helps to build rapport. It gives the person a greater sense of being understood. It is very useful when you want to influence them as you are quite literally 'talking their language'. You are influencing them in the way in which they prefer to think.

It is rather like using French to sell to someone from France and English to sell to someone from England. While your French customer can understand and speak English, they find it easier if you sell to them in French. On the other hand your English customer can also speak and understand French. However, it feels more natural and therefore easier for them if you sell to them in English.

Using someone's preferred representational system is a very powerful way of not only establishing and building rapport but also easing communication. It helps you to get your message across, and as a result close more sales.

Energy

You can also mirror someone's energy level – if they are very energetic and upbeat then you act likewise. If they are very relaxed and laid back than you become relaxed and laid back too.

When these actions are done carefully and elegantly they will be out of the other person's conscious awareness. Mirroring someone is not the same as mimicry. It is a subtle process. It should be done from an attitude of respect. You are attempting to establish rapport so that your communication and relationship with the other person is as good as it can possibly be.

Establishing rapport can build a sense of trust very quickly. You have a responsibility to use it carefully and ethically. It can also lead you to sharing the other person's experiences and should therefore be used with care.

Pace and Lead

A powerful way to influence people is to match, pace and lead. Initially you would match or mirror their posture, vocal qualities and energy level. You would also 'speak their language' using their preferred representational system. You would then continue to do this on an ongoing basis during the interaction. This is known as pacing.

It is as though you are having a conversation with someone while out walking. You need to move at the same pace as them for the conversation to be possible.

Leading is when you take them where *you* want to go. It is also the test to check if you have established rapport. After pacing them you can attempt to lead. Make a physical movement such as a change of posture. If within thirty to sixty seconds they have unconsciously followed your lead you can be confident that you have established rapport. It can be very entertaining to practice this technique and see just what you can get people to do!

Leading is not confined to physical movements or postures. You can lead vocally and energetically by starting to put more excitement and energy into your voice. Combining these elements together is a very powerful way to change your customer's state!

For example, having paced for a while you could start to gradually increasing the speed and enthusiasm of your voice, and then lean forward to look at the sales proposal on the desk in front of you. As you have established rapport the customer will start to feel more enthusiastic about your proposal and will also lean forward to take a closer look! If this is done subtly and with care it is a very, very influential technique.

Pacing Current Reality

Another powerful way that you can use the concept of pacing and leading is to do what is know as 'pacing current reality'. This simple and powerful method involves making statements about the current reality to your customer before directing their attention somewhere else. For example:

"Mr Customer, you are sitting in your chair in your office, listening to me and you know that like lots of other companies in your industry, you need to do something to increase your sales."

If you re read the sentence above you will see that it is a mixture of things that are true and a statement that is suggestive:

"You are sitting in your chair" (true), "in your office" (true), "listening to me" (true), "and you know that like lots of other companies in your industry you need to do something to increase your sales" (suggestion).

My intention with this sentence is to get the customer into a state of mind where they are thinking about needing to increase their sales. In this example, I would be intending to follow this up with a discussion about how I can help them to do just that! I will be more likely to succeed if I get them into the correct frame of mind first.

I use this technique when running training programmes for sales people too. Here's another example:

"Good morning, welcome to Sedgebrook Hall. Well done for finding your way here, it is a rather rural location, and here we all are in the Oak Suite for the Bare Knuckle Selling programme, and I'm hoping that you are very curious about all the powerful techniques you are going to learn..."

I want to get my audience into a curious and receptive state of mind, and by breaking down the statement you will see the blend of true statements and suggestions:

"Good morning (true   it is morning!), "welcome to Sedgebrook Hall" (true   we are at Sedgebrook Hall). "it is a rather rural location" (true), "here we all are in the Oak suite for the Bare Knuckle Selling programme" (true) and "you are very curious about all the powerful techniques that you are going to learn." (suggestion!)

A very similar structure to the above forms the basis of a method that hypnotists use when getting their clients into a hypnotic trance. It is a subtle and powerful technique to use whenever you are persuading.

Summary

If you use the techniques and methods described in this chapter, you will have made a powerful first impression on your customer, you will have grabbed their attention and made them interested to talk to you, and you will have established a good level of rapport with them. This provides a strong foundation upon which you can build the rest of your sales call.

Mining For Gold!

Step 4 of the Bare Knuckle Selling process: "Understanding Customer Needs and Criteria"

If I had to emphasise one step in the sales call to sales people, it would be this – understanding customer needs and criteria. Your first job as a salesperson is to understand *exactly* what it is that a customer needs. Once you have done that you can ascertain if your product or service can satisfy those needs. If it can, then you explain to the customer how their needs are met by the unique characteristics of your product or service. That, in a nutshell is what selling *should* be about.

As simple and straightforward as this concept is, it is surprisingly rare to find many sales people who follow its principles. Most sales people get it the wrong way around. They tell prospects and customers all about their products and services in the hope that they'll like it. Their focus is on *their* products and services rather than the customer's *needs*. This is a big mistake to make.

As a sales person your job is to focus your attention on the customer. You must focus on what is important to them. By doing this you can gather information on what they need, and then you can help them to get it. It helps to think about it as the selling equivalent of a very thorough medical examination! You examine the customer's situation thoroughly and carefully and then make a considered recommendation.

Selling this way makes the whole process so much easier. It is also makes it a more pleasant experience for the person being sold to. When you have been sold to by a professional, you feel great about your decision!

Perhaps you can recall a time when a salesperson talked *at* you about their products or services? Can you remember how annoying and frustrating it was? Perhaps you can recall a time when a sales person droned on and on about their product without pausing for feedback? They probably told you a lot of information you just didn't need to know.

I was recently buying a computer and endured a twenty minute monologue from a sales person in a well known computer store. I didn't get the chance to speak once! He droned on and on about all the technical data that wasn't of the slightest interest to me. Not once did he even think to ask me what I wanted to do with the computer!

Towards the end of his presentation I wasn't just starting to lose the will to buy a computer, I was starting to lose the will to live!

Contrast this with the highly professional salesman who separated my wife and I from several thousand pounds in return for a state of the art home cinema system. He asked us a lot of questions about what we were looking for, provided relevant advice and continued to ask questions throughout our conversation. We knew we wanted to buy a home cinema system (I'm a big movie fan), and he helped us to buy the one that was exactly right for us. End result? We have a home cinema system we absolutely love and he has earned a sizeable chunk of commission. A win win outcome.

I often refer to this stage of the selling process as 'mining for gold'. Through a structured conversation with the customer you uncover their exact needs. These are like precious nuggets of gold. Collect enough of them and you will close the sale easily!

What Are Needs?

Needs are things that people and businesses require. We can think about needs in a commercial context as being structured as a pyramid. At the top of the pyramid is what could be called the primary or ultimate business need.

The Primary Or Ultimate Business Need

The primary function of any commercial organisation is to make a profit. Profit therefore, is top of the pyramid.

Supporting Needs

Supporting the achievement of profit are the three drivers of profit. These are:

1. The number or volume of items you sell

2. The price you sell the items at

3. The margin you make when you sell them

No matter what business you are in this formula will apply. Profit will always be a result of how many things you sell (be that hours of work or product units), the price you sell them at and the margin you make (fundamentally this is the difference between what you sell it for and what it cost you to supply it to the customer).

So for example, in order to increase profits a customer may have a need to sell more of their products, increase the price they sell them for, or to enhance their margin through things like improving their buying price or operating their business more efficiently.

Customer-Specific Needs

The primary need and the supporting need are supported further down the pyramid with unique business needs. Every business is different and as a result will have unique needs. These are often the needs that will, if satisfied, result in enhancements to volume, price and margin and ultimately profit.

These could include: enhancements to the range of products stocked, greater efficiency, reducing the number of employees required, the ability to be competitive on price, increased customer footfall, promotional activity, enhanced customer loyalty, lower marketing and promotional cost etc.

It is said that there are only really four ways to grow a business:

1. Find new customers for your products and services
2. Get existing customers to buy more frequently
3. Get customers to spend more on each transaction
4. Reduce the cost of supplying the goods and services

Therefore, many of the needs that you will uncover will fall into one of these four categories. Uncovering how these specifically apply to your prospect or customer gives you highly valuable information that you can use to further focus your benefits on your customer's situation. Without this knowledge you will be shooting in the dark.

Personal Needs

The base of our needs pyramid are the personal needs of the people involved. Although there are many theories of personal needs a useful framework is:

Survival Needs

The need to have food, water and shelter is a fundamental and powerful need that people have. It is thankfully rare for people to starve to death in the developed world and this can perhaps cause people to dismiss these survival needs as being of little importance in a sales situation.

However, socio analytical theory states that a deep driver at an unconscious level is the desire to achieve some status and therefore some control over these resources. This desire may be driven by deep seated unconscious needs.

It would therefore be a mistake to dismiss the effect that these needs have on people. These needs can make themselves apparent in all sorts of selling situations. It may not be as extreme as the need to get food in order to survive, but if you consider it from the need to gain control over important resources it can help to explain what drives some people's behaviour.

Emotional Needs

There are some common emotional needs that most people have. Building on the previous comments around exerting some control over resources there is the need for:

Certainty

People need a certain amount of the familiar and predictable in their lives.

This may be linked to the certainty over controlling resources. The need for the familiar exerts a powerful effect over people and can be a powerful need to tap into. Perhaps driven by this need people can have a fear of the unknown and of making mistakes.

Variety

Conversely, people also need a certain amount of variety in their lives. Without some degree of change and diversity life could be pretty dull. This need is more pronounced in some people than others, but it is a useful one to tap into!

Significance

Once again, perhaps linked to being able to control resources, people have a need to become significant. This need manifests itself in the purchase of goods such as luxury cars, designer clothing, expensive property and so on. Linked to this, people may also have a need to feel clever or superior, and the need to make smart moves. This need also manifests when people fear feeling stupid or being seen to make a mistake.

Connection and Love

The final area of emotional need is that of social contact. Connection with others and receiving affection and love is very important to nearly all of us. You can observe this powerful need manifesting when people shop for attractive clothes, make up, dating agencies, diets, networking with others and so on.

Fulfilment Needs

Finally, people have a need to gain meaning and purpose in their lives. They have a need to grow as an individual. In addition, many people have a need to contribute beyond themselves. They need to make a difference to other people's lives and perhaps to leave a legacy. These needs can manifest themselves as charitable work, self development, mentoring, coaching, 'giving something back', parenting and so on.

Needs are a very powerful and essential thing to uncover as part of the selling process. At this stage it is important to discuss a distinction.

The Difference Between Wants And Needs

To be a highly effective salesperson you need to understand the difference between a want and a need. A want is something a prospect or customer desires. A need is something, that if truly satisfied will bring genuine benefit to them.

To return to my story where Martin advised us on our mortgage options, what we *wanted* was to change our mortgage. What we *needed* in order to get the most financial benefit was to wait for several months, allow our current agreement to expire and then to sign up for a new mortgage.

In the same way, your customers may have an idea about what they want to purchase. Your job as a salesperson is to find out if what they *want* is, in fact, what they *need*. Will what they want really bring them the maximum benefit?

We will return to this concept later. The full process that you will learn is to understand what a customer wants, make sure that this is what they really need and then sell them on *wanting* what they need. This is called the 'wants – needs – wants' process. When done effectively this is a very powerful process that will result in many sales.

To really close sales consistently your customers must not only need your product or service, they must want it and they must be motivated to buy it.

Bring On The Pain!

Human beings can be thought of as being motivated by two things:

1. The desire to gain pleasure
2. The desire to avoid pain

While the desire to gain pleasure can be a powerful motivating factor, in my experience, people (in general) are even more motivated to avoid pain. Pain (or at least the fear of pain) can often be the thing that motivates people to take action, to move out of inertia, to actually do something!

Many people have a tendency to procrastinate. Focusing the prospect or customer on their pain can be just the thing to get them to take action. Nobody really wants to procrastinate and a good selling process can help people to overcome their procrastination.

Pain, in this context, does not necessarily refer to avoiding physical pain. Pain can be thought of as a more general discomfort that may manifest itself mentally, emotionally or financially. Another way of framing pain is as the problems that your customers might experience.

Examples could be:

- Advertising that doesn't get the desired response
- Losing customers to the competition
- Struggling to find new customers
- Too much work to do
- Working too many hours
- Big tax bills that eat into profits
- New competitors appearing on the scene
- and so on...

Problems like these can motivate your customers to take action. Your job as a sales person is, by skilful questioning and effective listening, to uncover the problems your prospects and customers are experiencing. You can then demonstrate how your products and services can help to overcome the issues they are facing.

When this 'pain/problem', or as it is sometimes described 'away from' motivation is combined with pleasurable, 'towards' motivation, you will have created a powerful motivating force that gets people eager to buy from you.

When a customer really needs your product or service both of you will benefit from your ability to convince him to buy it.

The process is as follows:

1. Understand the current context for your customer. You need to understand the ins and outs of their business or life.

2. Ask questions to elicit the problems and/or pain the customer is currently experiencing.

3. Ask questions to ensure the customer fully appreciates the longer term consequences of not doing something about their current situation. For example, not making adequate pension arrangements before your forties, makes it highly unlikely that when you retire your pension will allow you to enjoy a comfortable retirement.

   To add impact you can explore current problems and future consequences. In my experience it is usually the pain that the person is currently experiencing that are the greatest motivator.

4. Ask question to elicit the positive or pleasurable outcomes the customer wants to enjoy instead.

5. Demonstrate how your product or service will help to solve their problems *and* deliver the pleasure (positive outcome) they desire.

If you master this process you will be amazed at how easily you can close so many more sales than you did before. So don't be squeamish: bring on the pain and then show them the pleasure.

The Power Of Criteria

As well as having needs, people also have other things that are important to them. At a high level, these are referred to as 'values' (freedom, security, achievement, adventure etc).

At a more specific level, people also have 'values' within a given context. These values are called 'criteria'. Criteria are context dependant. They can be elicited by asking, "What is important to you..." For example, "What is important to you when choosing a supplier?", "What is important to you in a new car?", "What is important to you about a holiday?"

The answers that you get (reliability, flexibility, responsiveness, excitement, fun, performance etc.) are valuable things to know, as in a situation where you wish to influence someone, they can be a person's 'hot buttons'.

Press these 'hot buttons' and you will get a powerful response!

So if you asked a potential customer what was important to them when choosing a new supplier, and they replied, "reliability, flexibility and responsiveness" you would be strongly advised to weave the fact that you are 'reliable, flexible and responsive' into your sales presentation!

Compare the power of this approach of establishing needs and criteria with the amateur salesperson who drones on and on about how amazing their product or service is before understanding anything about what is important to the customer.

By following the Bare Knuckle Selling approach you will leave these amateur sales people choking in your dust!

So what does it take to understand your customer's needs? Here are a selection of tools...

Two Vital Skills of The Sales Professional

I cannot emphasise enough the importance of *asking really good questions* and then *listening carefully* to your customer's responses. The ability to question and listen is so very important. Despite this fact, it is very rare to find anyone who was taught how to do this in school! Perhaps this is the reason why so many people are bad at it.

Please take plenty of time to focus on this area, as it is so very important.

Listening

The good news is that from my experience of training more sales people than I care to remember, I have never found anyone who cannot listen well. Perhaps I should qualify that – I have never found anyone who cannot listen well, when they focus their attention and concentration upon listening.

Too many sales people are so busy talking about their products and services, and thinking about what they're going to say next, that they never get around to doing any listening at all. It is very difficult to listen to what someone is saying if you are blathering.

Subtle hint: Shut your mouth and open your ears!

It is interesting to note that the very same letters that make up the word listen – L I S T E N also make up the word silent – S I L E N T.

L – I S – T – E – N

S – I – L – E – N – T

So, if you want to be a good listener you need to learn to close your mouth. However, there is a little bit more to it than just keeping your mouth shut.

You need to be concentrating and focusing your attention on what the other person is saying. One of the things that can really interfere with this is if you are busy chattering away to yourself inside your own head. If, while the other person is talking, you are busy thinking about what you are going to say next, then you aren't really listening are you?

It is sometimes said that a salesperson's definition of listening is, "what you do while you are waiting to say something else!" This is not what the salesperson's definition of listening should be. Your definition of listening is ensuring you fully understand what is important to the other person.

Blocks To Good Listening

Let us now explore some of the reasons for poor listening:

Lack of Attention

Your focus and concentration are not on the person speaking but on something else.

Jumping to Conclusions

As the other person is speaking, you make an assumption about what the person needs before you fully understand. This is a major fault of many sales people. I once witnessed this in a BMW garage. I was about to place an order for a brand new BMW. I knew exactly the model I wanted but I also wanted to check out some options for the interior. My wife and I had been clearing some junk out of our garage and on the way back from the rubbish tip we dropped in to ask a few questions. Karen and I were standing by the car in the showroom looking inside it when the sales man walked up. Catching sight of our rather scruffy attire (we don't usually wear our smartest clothes when cleaning out the garage and going to the tip) he said in an arrogant and superior tone of voice, "Just looking, right?" Wrong! Just about to hand over a big chunk of cash on a brand new BMW actually. But due to your condescending and arrogant attitude not with you, you (expletive deleted)! One conclusion jumped to, one big sale and accompanying commission lost. I eventually placed the order with another dealer.

Perhaps we have just had unfortunate encounters with car sales people, but a further example of jumping to conclusions was when Karen was buying a new car and I went along for the ride. I take every opportunity to see sales people in action – I am always interested to learn new ways of improving my selling.

Karen was really interested in buying a Volkswagen Golf, and the salesperson at the dealership was showing us a few options. The mistake he made was to look at Karen when he mentioned anything to do with colour, interior, the CD player etc and towards me when he mentioned anything 'technical' such as details about the engine.

This was a big mistake. Firstly, I was only along for the ride. Karen was the one making the decision, not me. Secondly, my technical knowledge of cars is limited to where to stick the fuel. I once took a car back to the garage complaining that the dipstick was too short to reach the oil!

Before she met me, Karen had a partner who was an expert on cars. He was a racing driver in his spare time and Karen was often roped in to do work on his racing car. My wife can strip down a car engine faster than most people can eat their breakfast! There isn't a lot she doesn't know about car engines, so to treat her as if she is ignorant of such things, just because she is a woman is a rather stupid thing for a salesperson to do. If he had avoided jumping to conclusions he could have enjoyed spending the commissions he made on the sale. However, it was another sale down the drain! The amount of money sales people are losing through this sort of behaviour must run into hundreds of millions of pounds a year!

Assuming People Think Like You Do

If you make the mistake of assuming other people think like you do, you make many, many mistakes and lose too many sales. A 'boy racer' car salesman will not sell many cars to safety conscious people if all he talks about is how amazingly fast the car can accelerate.

Excessive Talking

As discussed above, this is when you are so busy broadcasting when you should be receiving. Stop it – it annoys customers!

Lack of Humility

This is when a touch of over confidence rears its ugly head and you assume you have the answer to all of your customer's problems, without really understanding them in the first place. If a sales person who does not understand what I want starts to use phrases such as, "I can tell you this is what you want" or, "What you want is...", I mentally line them up for a sharp right hook!

Fear

Sometimes sales people are so scared that the customer might say something that will be unhelpful to them selling something, that they don't give the customer the chance to talk! If they were to shut up and listen then they would discover valuable information that could help them sell effectively. If someone has no need of your product or service then find out quickly and move onto someone who does.

Please don't make these mistakes – they will cost you money!

A Powerful Technique To Help Your Listening

A simple, but powerful method of improving your listening is called 'rapid repeat'. With rapid repeat you simply repeat what the other person has said to yourself, inside your own head a fraction of a second after they have said it.

In this way you actually get to hear what is being said twice – once when the prospect or customer actually says the words and secondly as you repeat them to yourself. In addition, the act of focusing your attention upon the words and repeating them prevents you from distracting yourself with your own internal dialogue and thoughts.

This is a deceptively simple technique and I would recommend that you practice it and use it.

Questions

The partner to effective listening is effective questioning. The two go together like a hand in a glove!

You use questions to understand your customer's situation. You use questions to elicit your customer's needs, wants and criteria. You use questions to get your customer to appreciate the implications of not taking action.

Compare this approach to the amateur sales person who just *tells* the customer about their products.

Telling is not selling!

Asking questions and listening carefully to the answers is selling.

The Four Types Of Questions

Broadly speaking there are four types of questions that you can use in a selling situation. These are:

- Closed
- Open
- Probing
- Summarising

These can be remembered by way of the handy mnemonic C.O.P.S.

CLOSED QUESTIONS

These are used to obtain a specific answer and to check facts. Examples would include:

"Was it a success?"

"Is that important to you?"

"Does anyone else need to approve this?"

Closed questions usually result in a "yes" or "no" answer.

OPEN QUESTIONS

These are broad, diagnostic questions that encourage the customer to talk about their situation. Open questions usually start with words such as what, when, why, how, where, who, which and usually result in a multi word or sentence answer.

Examples would include:

"What do you want to change or improve about your business?"

"What don't you like about your current supplier?"

"How do you currently handle customer complaints?"

"Why are you considering a new car?"

It is important to stress that open questions usually result in a multi word/sentence answer and closed questions usually result in a single word answer. However, in many cases you can get a "yes" or "no" to a good open question and a long reply to a closed question!

Some sales trainers place so much emphasis on 'open questions' (which we'll cover next) that using 'closed questions' appears to be one of the seven deadly sins. This is utter rubbish. Both open and closed questions have their place in the selling process.

Open questions are used to gather information and closed questions are used to clarify what you discover and get specific answers and commitments.

PROBING QUESTIONS

These are used to explore a point a customer has made. They allow you to drill further into what the customer has said so that you can understand it in more detail.

Examples include:

"What makes you say that?"

"In what way do you think...?"

"Give me an example of...?"

"How do you mean?"

"Why did you bring that up?"

A useful probing technique is to use 'echo questions'. An echo question is where you use the last word or few words of what the customer says as a probing question.

An example:

"We need a supplier who is reliable."

"Reliable?"

In this example, you are probing further to discover how the customer defines 'reliable'. If you did not probe, you could make some assumptions about what 'reliable' means to you.

SUMMARISING QUESTIONS

These are used to sum up the conversation you have had with the customer and to confirm the discussion you have had so far. This helps to keep the sales call on track and to check and clarify understanding.

Examples include:

"So if I understand correctly, what you are saying is...?"

"So have we agreed that...?"

Combining Your Questions Into A Funnel

A very elegant method of really understanding what your customer wants, needs and values is to combine questions in a funnel. You start with broad information at the top of the funnel and using a combination of open, probing, summarising and closed questions you get very specific information at the bottom.

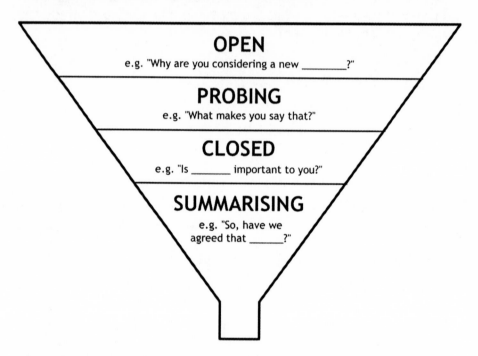

At the broad, top of the funnel you ask lots of 'open questions' that encourage the customer to tell you about their situation and what is important to them.

You then use 'probing questions' to gather more information about specific areas.

You can use 'closed questions' to clarify information and check specific facts and 'summarising questions' to wrap up the questioning process.

You can use a series of funnels to gather all of the information you need to fully understand the customer's needs, wants and criteria.

Once you have done this you are in a position to move to the next stage of the selling process.

The art of asking questions and listening carefully is what separates the professional sales people from the amateurs. I cannot emphasise enough the difference between a professional Bare Knuckle Seller and the amateur seller:

- Amateur sellers give their customers a good *talking* to.

- Professional Bare Knuckle Sellers give their customers a good *listening* to!

Show Me The Money!

Step 5 of the Bare Knuckle Selling process: "Understand The Customer's Budget"

When I am training sales people they sometimes express concern that I advocate raising the subject of money so early in a sales call. There is a school of thought that states that you should only mention money when you have presented your product or service to the customer and shown them how it will benefit them. The belief is that you need to cushion the price by demonstrating its value before you mention it.

It is a very good idea to strongly communicate to the customer the value they are getting in return for the price that they are paying. However, I have some very good reasons for advising you to raise the subject of money at this stage in the sales call.

Firstly, there is always an air of tension during a sale before the customer knows what the price is. I believe that this takes the customer's attention away from the sale. When I was buying double glazing for my house, I was distracted from the sales person presentation about how great their windows were, because I didn't know how much they were going to cost and I wanted to know!

Secondly, this stops people wasting your time. Face the harsh facts: if a very helpful salesperson offers plenty of free advice and consultancy in the hope of getting a sale, there are people that are quite happy to take advantage of this!

These people will bleed you dry for advice and free information. If they just don't have the money to afford your services, or have no intention of paying any way, then you will just turn into a free advice bureau for them. I am not saying that you shouldn't use things like free taster sessions as a stage in selling your products or services. But I am saying that you need to know if people have the money to pay you early on!

Thirdly, you need to know what sort of solution the customer is looking for. Recently I was looking for a provider to train a team of trainers to be more effective executive coaches. I contacted a guy who came highly recommended. We arranged to meet up and we discussed what I was looking for. I was the one who raised the subject of price. The gentleman concerned said that he wasn't cheap. His rate per day was £3,000. I was comfortable with his day rate as I knew he was very good. We discussed arranging a few days training for the team of trainers and he said that he would submit a proposal.

When the proposal arrived I was in for a shock. Firstly, he had not listened to what I wanted. I wanted three or four days training for the team. They were, as I had explained to him, already familiar with coaching and wanted to enhance their skills. Secondly, he had not discussed my budget. I was expecting a fee of between £9,000 and £12,000.

His proposal was for £85,000! He had decided that he needed to run an in depth diagnostic process on a one to one basis with each trainer, to run a seven day coaching skills workshop and then provide several days one to one coaching support to each of the team afterwards. I phoned him up, politely told him that he was having a laugh and placed the business with another provider.

Fourthly, you need to know how you are getting paid. You need to understand under what terms and conditions payment will be made. A sale is not a sale until the money is in your bank account. Professional sales people make sure they get paid!

After you have completed the process of understanding your customer's need, wants and criteria you need to talk money. If you have completed the last stage of the call successfully, you not only understand their needs, wants and criteria, you will also have made them appreciate their pain and problems more acutely. You have them motivated to do something about it.

This is the time to ask, "Mr Customer, do you have a budget set aside for this?" or "Mr Customer, do you have a budget to solve this problem?" The customer can only really respond in one of two ways – yes or no!

If it is a "Yes" then this is wonderful! You can ask, "Would you mind sharing it with me?" Sometimes a customer will reply that they cannot or will not share the budget with you. If this happens then say, "Yes, I understand" or "Okay that makes sense." Then make a further attempt to understand their budget with, "I appreciate that, can you let me know some round numbers?" This softens the request and makes it seem less imposing.

You can follow this by saying, "Mr Customer we have solutions to your sort of problem that range from £5,000 to £25,000 (or whatever price range you work within). The reason I ask is because we can solve most problems but some cost £5,000 and some cost £25,000. I understand your desire for confidentiality but should we address this as a £5,000 or a £25,000 solution?"

This will often result in the customer disclosing a figure, or at the very least giving you some guidance as to a "ballpark" amount.

If the reply is "No" then you can reply, "Well that's not unusual. How do you plan to move this forward?" I appreciate that this approach may seem to be rather bold, but it is designed to (amongst other things) flush out if the customer is really serious about going ahead and spending some money, or if they are just looking for some free help.

Sometimes the customer will respond with a figure that is on the low side. Sometimes this is done as a negotiation ploy. They hope that by starting with a low figure that they will get a cheaper price.

The counter to this is to say, "Hmmm. That could be a bit of a problem. I don't think we are going to be able to go first class on this one. Are there some things we could trim off if we need to?"

This communicates that you have a confidence in your self, your product or service, and that the only way you will be able to meet the customer's low budget is by tailoring your product or service in some way to meet this. In my experience this approach often results in the available budget increasing! On the other hand if that really is the budget your customer has, then you are able to either tailor your offering or move onto more profitable customers.

Occasionally, following the Bare Knuckle Selling approach will result in some sales not going ahead. The good news is that these are ones that are likely to be low in profitability. In addition, you will spend less time chasing after people who are very unlikely to buy from you anyway. Time is money – the more time you spend with people who are going to buy, the more money you make.

Decisions, Decisions

The other important element at this stage of the sale is to understand how the customer will make their decision. You must understand how the decision making process will work.

In the commercial world, all propositions require someone to make a decision. Increasingly, in the business environment, decisions are made by groups of people rather than by one individual.

If you are selling straight to the consumer then you need to be aware that this can also apply. For any 'big ticket' purchases such as cars, property, investments, mortgages, holidays, education, double glazing, kitchens, furniture, garden landscaping, major home improvements, expensive electronic goods and so on, it is rare for the decision to be made by just one person. The other partner, their children or even parents may be involved. Often both partners in a relationship will be involved in the final decision. One partner may have more influence and sway over the decision but it is unwise to discount the other people involved.

In our family Karen will often do most of the research into a big ticket purchase (I'm usually very busy selling, honest!) and then involve me in the final decision. She is firmly in the driving seat on most occasions and I respect and value her judgement, but it would be unwise for a sales person to assume that I have *no* influence.

It is unwise to ignore the influence of every person involved in the sale. Even grown adults often ask their parents for advice before making major decisions!

We recently purchased a new bed for our young son Thomas. We were very keen on a wonderful bunk bed with a big comfortable chair and desk underneath. The wise salesman in the furniture shop involved Thomas in the selling process. He invited Tom to climb onto the bed and asked him what he thought. He also asked Tom a few questions about what he liked doing, and when he discovered his love of Play Station, he said that Tom could put his Play Station on the desk under the bed and play it while sitting in the big comfortable chair. Tom was sold! Karen and I also liked the idea of transforming Tom and his friends' 'Play Station Room' back into the dining room it was supposed to be! The wise sales person moved swiftly and efficiently to get us to sign the order. The particular brand of beds in question cost well over £1000 each, so involving the whole family in the sale is a must in a market where other similar beds are available for a fraction of the price.

In a business context you need to be aware of four types of people in a decision making process:

1. Decision Influencers

These are the individuals (or groups of individuals) who want to be involved or whom the decision maker wants to be involved. Usually if they say "no" that means "no". However, it does not follow that if they say "yes" that they mean "yes".

2. Decision Makers

These are the individuals (or groups of individuals) who weigh all of the available information and options and who make the final decision.

3. Decision Owners

This is the individual (or individuals) who takes 'ownership' of the decision and is accountable for the results.

4. Implementers

These are the individuals who make the "yes" decision a reality.

You need to understand who will be involved in the decision making process and understand the role that they will play.

By way of example, I was once selling an expensive concept to a company with over 400 retail outlets. I was successful in getting a slot at their board meeting to get the final agreement to proceed.

I had already convinced the Head Buyer that it was a good thing to do. He would be one of the owners of the decision. The Retail Operations Director would also be a 'decision owner'. I spent time with him to sell him on the idea also. I knew that the board would ask him for his opinion. He would be a 'decision influencer' too. If he said "yes" this would be a positive step forward but would not guarantee the sale. However, if he said "no" I would be out of the door with no sale.

The team who reported into the Retail Director would be the people who would make the decision become a reality if I got the go ahead. I arranged to meet them at a team meeting to discuss the proposal and get their views.

In addition, it was likely to be the CEO of the organisation who gave the final approval to go ahead. My buyer arranged a meeting for us with the CEO. We succeeded in gaining his agreement to go ahead if the rest of the board approved of the proposal.

On the day of the board meeting my buyer introduced me, and I made my presentation. At one stage the main Finance Director turned to the Retail Director (decision influencer) and asked him his opinion. The Retail Director gave the proposal his support and I continued my presentation. After I had finished I was asked a number of questions and then it went quiet for a moment or two as the board contemplated my proposal.

I took the opportunity to make eye contact with the CEO and raised my eyebrows in an enquiring manner, prompting him to say something. He then spoke up and said that he thought that they should proceed with the proposal. He asked for thoughts from the other board members. Due to his influential position in the organisation this guided the other board members to approve the proposal and the sale was in the bag!

Had I not ensured that all of the key people involved in the decision making process were involved, the result may not have been so favourable.

A good way to work out the entire decision making process is to ask, "What is the decision making process that you follow?" or "Who, besides yourself, is involved in making this decision?"

If the customer replies that he makes all decisions on his own, it can pay to gently check this out. You need to be careful not to cause any offence, but it is very rare that just one person is involved in making significant commercial decisions!

A gentle way to check this out is to say, "You mean if you wanted to do it today, you could do it?" or "Wow! You mean you don't get any help with this?" Asking such questions will often elicit some comment from the customer about other people who are involved.

The MAP Check

Before you leave this step of the sales call, it is useful to check that you have achieved the following:

M - Money

Have you established that the customer has the budget to proceed?

Do you know how much the budget is?

Do you know how to get the money; do you need a purchase order number, will they pay by credit card etc?

A - Authority

Do you know who has the authority to make the decision?

Who are the decision influencers, makers, owners and implementers?

P - Pain

Do you fully understand the customer's problems and pain?

To move on in the sales call from here it is important to review progress so far. Please move to the next chapter where we shall do exactly that!

The First Pivot Point

Step 6 of the Bare Knuckle Selling process: "Get the Agreement to Proceed"

Although this is a small section of the sales call (and therefore a short chapter) this is a very important, and often overlooked, part of the selling process.

Far too many sales calls lack structure, pace and purpose. The call meanders around and as a result it takes far too long. In today's busy world people just do not have time to waste.

This step of the sales call reviews progress so far and signals to the customer that the call is about to change format and pace.

This step is very important as you will use it to clarify that you:

1. Understand the customer's needs, wants and criteria (including the pain and problems they are experiencing)

2. Understand the available budget

Then having received confirmation from the customer that you are correct, you will gain the customer's agreement to proceed with your proposal.

You can only properly proceed with a proposal when, (as discussed in the last chapter) you understand the customer's MAP, that is:

*   Money – Available budget
*   Authority – Decision making process
*   Pain – the problems that the customer is experiencing

You do this by saying something like:

"Mr Customer, can I check my understanding of what we have discussed so far? My understanding is that you are concerned about (problem) and the effects it is having on your business. In addition you are worried about the longer term affect that (problem) will have on profitability. Is that right? Due to the potential financial impact of (problem) you are able to invest up to £10,000 to get this problem solved."

If you are getting agreement from the customer then you can proceed. Signs of agreement can be verbal responses like, "yes" or non verbal responses such as head nodding. If you are getting positive responses then it is time to proceed. If you get any negative responses then you need to go back to questioning the customer further so that you can understand more fully.

When you do get a full positive response you exit this stage of the sales call by saying something like, "Mr Customer, if I could show how we could address this issue for you, and show you how this will benefit your business, would you be interested to understand more?"

Dependant upon your product or service, you may need to revisit the customer when you have drafted a tailored proposal. In this case you need to make a further appointment right away. In many cases however, you will be able to proceed to the next step of the sales call: Proposal and Presentation.

Proposals & Presentations

Step 7 of the Bare Knuckle Selling process: "Propose and Present"

Phew! I can hear you breathe a sigh of relief – at last we are actually going to get around to selling something. At last Simon Hazeldine is going to let me talk to the customer about *my* product or service!

Yes – your chance has now arrived. However, when you make your sales presentation to the customer you will be doing so with a full understanding of:

- The customer's specific needs and criteria. Not just the needs and criteria that apply to all businesses or people in their situation, but their unique needs and criteria. Not the needs or criteria that you think or hope they have, but the ones that are specific to them.

- The customer's decision making process. You know what needs to be done to get a 'yes'.

- The money available to you for helping the customer get their problems solved and their needs met.

Contrast that with the way amateur sales people do it. They don't bother with all that planning, rapport and questioning nonsense. They just get stuck into the sale. These are the sales people that earn our profession its bad reputation. These are the people who annoy customers and waste their time. These are the people who dribble on about how great they, their company and its products or services are without ever checking to see if the customer needs them.

Let me give you a harsh dose of reality. Customers don't really care about you or your products or your services. They don't care about you or what you sell. They aren't interested in how many years you have been in business. They don't really care about how qualified or experienced you are. They are not actually very interested in *you* at all. They hear pretty much the same poor quality sales pitch from most of the sales people they meet. Telling is not selling. Repeat after me, "*Telling is not selling!*"

They are only really interested in one thing about you   how you are going to help them to get what *they* want. They are only interested in how you can *solve their problems* and get them all the good things they are after.

This may sound somewhat harsh, but by focusing your attention in this way you will maximise your chances of closing more and more sales.

So, when presenting your proposal to the customer, it is helpful if you imagine a big cartoon style thought bubble above their head containing the question, "What's in it for me?"

In this chapter we use the terms 'proposal' and 'presentation' in the following way. A proposal refers to the content of what you will be presenting to the customer. It will contain the information on your product or service and the benefits that this will bring the customer.

The presentation is the means by which you communicate the contents of your proposal. Both the proposal and the presentation are vitally important.

A good proposal that is poorly presented is unlikely to succeed, as is a poor proposal even if it is presented superbly well.

Your goal in this step of the sales call is to get the customer to say "yes" to your proposal. To do this you need to focus on some important factors.

Who Should You Be Presenting Your Proposal To?

From your earlier questioning you will have identified the decision makers, owners, implementers and influencers. You need to make sure that these people are prese   n be available during your presentation.

If you are selling directly to the public, you will need to consider that many people you are selling to will be in some form of relationship. Therefore you need to consider the involvement of the husband, wife, partner, boyfriend, girlfriend or 'significant other' in the decision making process. Many couples make significant decisions together, or at the very least both parties involved have some influence.

What Should Be In Your Proposal?

Here is a framework that you can use to create your proposal:

- The customer's problems

    o Including any financial costs that they will or may incur as a result of not taking any action to resolve the issue. Remember to include the impact of current costs as well as a longer term view. A £30k loss over three years feels more painful than a £10k loss over one year!

- The customer's needs

    o Include a clear business context (in commercial situations) that demonstrates that you understand their needs.

- The customer's criteria

    o As you will have elicited the customer's criteria you might as well use them! Not including these 'hot buttons' will seriously weaken your proposal.

- The features and benefits of your product or service (we'll talk about features and benefits later)

    o Include if possible hard numbers to show the value of your proposal

    o You must show very strongly how the benefits of your product or service solve the customer's problems and meet their needs.

o It is important to show as strongly as possible how uniquely you (and only you) are in a position to give the customer what they want. Far too many sales proposals contain benefits that almost any half decent company can provide. For example, in today's competitive commercial world, the ability to provide next day delivery is no longer anything very special. More often than not it is becoming expected.

You absolutely must stand out from the crowd! In competitive situations your proposal may be one of several being considered. So what makes yours different?

- Testimonials from existing clients

Research by Professor Robert Cialdini from Arizona State University has revealed a number of factors that are hugely influential in getting people to say 'yes' to proposals. These factors are also largely unconscious and automatic and therefore very powerful as tools for persuasion.

One of the six factors is what Cialdini calls 'Social Proof'. This is the influential effect of what other people are doing. If we see or hear of other people doing something then it influences us to do it too.

This is why testimonials from satisfied customers or stories about how existing customers have benefited from your product or service are highly influential. You simply must have them in your selling armoury.

With all of the stereotypical misconceptions about sales people that exist, who do you think a customer is more likely to believe? A salesperson or a satisfied customer?

Another of Cialdini's six factors is the influence of 'Authority'. People in authority positions are seen as being far more believable than people who are not. Hence the reason that I mentioned that Cialdini is in fact Professor Cialdini! A Professor is a more influential authority figure than some bloke from your local pub. You can utilise this factor by positioning yourself as the authority in your chosen field or gaining testimonials from other authorities too.

I am reliably informed that writing a book is a good way of establishing this authority as author = AUTHORity. This therefore means that having written this book I am now more influential than ever before! Wow this authorship stuff is good!

- The financial investment (please note the use of the word 'investment' rather than 'price' as it is a softer and more positive word to describe the money that customer will have to pay) required from the customer

  o You need to strongly demonstrate how the value that your proposal brings to the customer (in solving their problems and helping them get what they want) far outweighs the cost.

    This approach will help to counter any issues you may experience about the price of your product or service. A printing machine that costs £50k would seem expensive. However if I was to tell you that it was able to print perfectly legal £50 notes at a rate of £5000 per day, you would probably see it as a bargain and place your order immediately.

    In the same way, you need to demonstrate that the cost of your product or service is outweighed by the value it brings to the customer.

    Incidentally if anyone does manufacture the above printing machines could they please get in touch as I am willing to offer my sales services for a very reasonable commission on every order taken!

- A clear action plan, implementation plan and motivation to action

  o It is very important that your proposal includes a strong call to action. This prevents the sales call from fizzling out. Far too many sales dwindle and die due to a weak action plan/implementation plan or the lack of a strong call to action.

Presenting Your Proposal

Now that you have your proposal you will need to present it to the customer.

If you recall we are making sure that you get a big tick in both boxes for:

- What you say
- How you say it

So having devised a killer proposal we are going to present it to the customer in such a powerful way that it blows their socks off!

Keep It Simple, Clear And Concise

Having coached sales people for many years on their proposals and presentation skills, I can report that there are usually three common problems. Far too many sales presentations are:

1. Too long
2. Too boring
3. Too self indulgent

We live in a busy modern world. Keeping your sales presentations as brief as possible (but no briefer) and to the point will help you avoid taking up too much of the customer's time and annoying them.

You must keep focused on what is in it for the customer. Keep your focus off yourself and firmly on the customer. Far too many sales people are in love with their companies, products, services and perhaps themselves. As a result they talk too much about what they are interested in, thinking that the customer will be interested too.

Features and Benefits

If you have ever been fortunate enough to experience any form of sales training then you will most certainly have been exposed to the concept of features and benefits. Feature and benefit selling has been around for over 50 years. As a result most sales people have heard about it or have been trained in it.

Due to this fact, when I am running sales training programmes and I mention features and benefits, almost everyone confirms that they know all about it. The participants will usually have done features and benefits before and aren't too interested to spend too much time on the subject.

What is fascinating though is that although they have *heard* of the concept and probably *understand* it, when these very same sales people take part in selling role plays, they don't seem to be able to *do* feature and benefit selling!

As a result of this, I now tell sales people that I know they know about features and benefits. What I am interested in is do they do it! So what is feature and benefit selling?

Features

A feature is a characteristic of a product or service. It is part of the intrinsic make up of the product or service. It explains what is different or better about the product or service.

Examples of features include: price, support, packaging, warranty, ingredients, technical specification, expertise, how long a company has been in business, market leadership, growth of a product in its category, easy to carry, ease of use, eye catching design, size, weight, cutting edge technology, national coverage and so on.

Sales people are usually very good at talking about their products or services. And, most of us have had the misfortune of being on the receiving end of a barrage of confusing technical information when trying to buy an item of electrical equipment or computer.

The salesperson will tell us about all of the features of the product. While this may (or may not be) interesting and useful, what we are really interested in is the benefits of these features.

Benefits

A benefit is a 'future favourable result' that is forecast or promised upon the customer taking certain action. Benefits answer questions such as:

"What's in it for me?"

"What does it do for me?"

"So what?"

Benefits show customers how the features of a product or service will help them to solve their problems, reduce or remove their pain and give them the pleasure they want.

The wise sales person uses the features of their product or service and then links these to the benefits these features will give the customer. For example:

Feature: "This new product fills a price point gap in your current range..."

Benefit: "...which will extend your customer offering and result in more sales."

Feature: "This new machine will automate what has previously been a manual process..."

Benefit: "...which means you need less staff, which means you save money on your wage bill."

Feature: "This new display unit is very eye catching..."

Benefit: "...which means you will get more impulse purchases."

The features of your product or service are important, however what is more important to your customer is the benefit that these features give them. That is what the customer is really interested in!

The Difference Between Real Benefits and Possible Advantages

An important point to note is that a benefit is only a benefit when it is related to an identified customer need. If it is not related to a specific customer need then it is at best a possible advantage that the customer may or may not find interesting.

To give a personal example, my wife and I were buying a new kitchen for a house that we once lived in. The house needed a new kitchen. However, we did not intend to be living in the house for very long. We did need to re do the kitchen in the meantime, and knew that a nice kitchen would help us to sell the house in the future.

We endured a rather painful sales presentation from one kitchen sales person who kept on stressing the 'high quality' of the kitchen units he had available and how they would last for over twenty years. He kept on stressing that in twenty years time they would still be as good as new.

I guess that this was quite impressive (if you find kitchen cupboards interesting which unfortunately I do not) but of absolutely no benefit to Karen and I. We were not going to be in the house in two years time, never mind in twenty years time! The salesperson would have been more successful if he had taken the time to understand our specific needs and then tailor the features and benefits of his products to match these.

Link Phrases

There are a number of link phrases that you can use to join features and benefits together in a smooth and effective way. Let us use the feature and benefit mentioned earlier to show how a variety of these can be used.

Feature: A new eye catching display unit.

Benefit: More impulse purchases.

- There is a new eye catching display unit **which gives you** more impulse purchases.
- There is a new eye catching display unit **which will give you** more impulse purchases.
- The new display unit is very eye catching, **therefore** you get more impulse purchases.
- The new eye catching display unit **enables you** to secure more impulse purchases.
- You get a new eye catching display unit **so** you get more impulse purchases.

- There is a new eye catching display unit **so you get** more impulse purchases.
- The products come with an eye catching display unit **resulting in** more impulse purchases.
- There is a new eye catching display unit **so that** you get more impulse purchases.
- You get a new eye catching display unit **which means that** you will enjoy more impulse purchases.

Using a variety of link phrases means that your feature and benefit presentation flows naturally and easily. You will be aware that you are operating to a proven structure, however your customer will feel that they are having the benefits of your product or service explained to them in a very personal and tailored way.

Weave In Your Customer's Criteria

We discussed earlier, the power of eliciting customer's criteria. When selling these criteria are the customer's 'hot buttons'. They are the things that are important to them in a specific context.

Weaving these into your sales presentation is a very powerful method of influence.

As part of your job to elicit the criteria you will have asked something like, "What's important to you about..." and the customer will have replied with their criteria. The exact words they used to describe their criteria will be very important to them – so remembering what they were should be important to you.

It is very powerful to use their *exact* criteria words and phrases. Do this in a subtle way and it is very influential. For example, if the customer has said that one of their criteria is that a supplier most have "relevant experience" then you could say, "We have experience that is relevant to this field". But that's not nearly as powerful as using their exact phrase. It is far better to use the specific words (in this case "relevant experience") than to substitute it with your own phrases such as "highly experienced", "very experienced" or "many years of experience". It is not that there is anything wrong with these phrases, it is just that they do not meet the customer's *specific* criteria. So saying, "We have relevant experience in this field." is far more powerful.

Showing how your products or services meet the customer's *specific* criteria, along with meeting their *specific* needs and solving their *specific* problems will result in many, many more sales!

Hypnotic Selling Techniques

The powerful techniques that I am now about to share with you, have largely been drawn from studies of highly influential people and the style of language that they use.

A common misconception is that people need to be 'asleep' or to have their eyes closed to be affected by hypnotic language. It is very possible to use hypnotic language in a very influential way when people are wide awake!

Another benefit of these influential techniques is that they are easy to use. You will be able to use them to add influence and power to your sales presentations.

Presuppositions

A presupposition is something that is assumed beforehand as the basis of, for example, an argument or in order to make sense of a statement. Presupposition is a form of language in which certain ideas or experiences are presumed *without being directly stated*.

For example the statement, "Have you stopped wasting time on unproductive sales calls?" presupposes that you have been wasting time on unproductive sales calls!

The great hypnotherapist Milton Erickson said, "The power of presuppositions is that they cannot be ignored, and, if used subtly create expectations for change that are outside or beyond the conscious mind." So presuppositions are unconsciously influential!

If you re read my introduction to 'Hypnotic Selling Techniques' then you will notice the use of the presupposition, "Another benefit of these influential techniques is that they are easy to use." This presupposes (amongst other things) that there are a number of benefits to these influential techniques. The fact that there are a number of benefits is presupposed.

Here are some examples of how you can weave presuppositions into your selling presentation:

"Another advantage that this product brings you is..."

Presupposition: This product has more than one advantage for you!

"One of main reasons that XYZ Company chose us as their supplier is..."

Presupposition: There are a number of reasons that XYZ company chose us as their supplier!

"Amongst the many benefits of this product is..."

Presupposition: This product has many benefits!

"When the product is installed you will notice that..."

Presupposition: You will install this product!

"Based upon what you have told me one of the things you will be interested in about our service is..."

Presupposition: "You will be interested in more than one thing about our service!

When you use presuppositions subtly your customers will not realise what you are doing. In addition, when you start using presuppositions you will discover that your sales presentations are even more influential than they were before!

Tag Questions Are Very Influential, Aren't They?

When you put a tag question onto the end of a sentence it makes it difficult to disagree with it, doesn't it? Using tag questions at the end of sentences makes it far easier for people to agree with you.

Examples of tag questions are:

- Isn't it?
- Aren't you?
- Doesn't it?
- Don't you?
- Can't you?
- Don't they?
- Can you not?
- Wouldn't he?

The use of a tag question introduces a negative into the situation and your neurology processes negative phrases differently from positive phrases. According to research unexplained negation seems to cause some confusion in the listener. The effect of this appears to make the suggestion that precedes the tag question more readily accepted.

You can weave tag questions throughout the selling process, and they are particularly useful during your presentation, for example:

"You can go ahead today, can't you?"

"I'm sure that you can see why we need to go ahead right now, can't you?"

"Your managing director would want you to do this, wouldn't he?"

"Its okay to make an important decision like this, is it not?"

You can add power to your tag questions by doing the following as you say them:

1. Nod you head slowly

2. Use a downward voice inflection or pitch

The slow head nod will frequently produce a similar non verbal response from the customer – particularly if you have established deep levels of rapport as discussed earlier. In addition, the suggestive nod of the head is often outside of the conscious awareness of the other person.

A level voice inflection gets processed as a statement, a rising voice inflection gets processed as a question and a downward voice inflection gets processed by people as a command!

Combine these together and you have selling dynamite, don't you?

"You can place the order now, (nodding head and using downward voice inflection) can't you?" Please take the time to practice using tag questions with a downward voice inflection. They are very influential, are they not?

Embedded Suggestions

It is possible to embed a suggestion within a larger sentence. For example, "As you are looking over the proposal, I'm hoping that <u>you want to place an order right now</u>, so that we can get the show on the road."

"Now that you have had chance to understand the benefits, I'm hoping that you want to <u>say yes</u> to the proposal."

I have embedded the suggestion "place an order right now" and "say yes" within the larger sentences above.

You can enhance the impact of your embedded suggestions by marking them out with some slightly different form of behaviour. For example, you can:

- Shift your voice tone by lowering or deepening the tonality for instance
- Pause slightly before and after saying the embedded suggestion
- Raise your eyebrows or make a physical gesture

In a selling situation I often use a raised finger and lower voice tone to mark out my embedded suggestions. Earlier in the selling process every time I ask the customer to do something I make the particular movement and use the voice tone. For example, I may say "Let's take a look at the proposal", lowering my voice tone slightly and raising my right index finger as I say "take a look at the proposal." The customer will usually comply with my request and I have established an association between the voice tone, raised finger and the customer complying with my request.

Then later in the sale I can repeat the same pattern, saying, "At this stage most of my customers just want to <u>buy, buy, buy</u>! Why don't we <u>go ahead right now</u>? If you <u>say yes</u> right <u>now</u> you can start enjoying the benefits sooner rather than later."

A useful variation on embedded suggestions is to utilise phonological ambiguity. A phonological ambiguity is a word that sounds the same but has different meanings.

When a phonological ambiguity is used the theory goes that your brain processes all the various meanings to make sense of what is being said. In this way, phonological ambiguities can be used as a tool of influence. A favourite example is to use the word 'by' as it has the same sound as the word 'buy'.

For example: "<u>By now</u> Mr Customer, I'm sure you can see the benefits of this proposal. A <u>by product</u> of this arrangement is the free service support. <u>By</u> the way, we can arrange delivery next week, if you go ahead right now."

I am sure you will have spotted the phonological ambiguities!

"<u>Buy now</u> Mr Customer, I'm sure you can see the benefits of this proposal, can't you? A <u>buy product</u> of this arrangement is the free service support. <u>Buy</u> the way, we can arrange delivery next week, if you go ahead right now."

And if we take a look at all of the suggestions embedded in the paragraph we have a truly influential collection, don't we?

"<u>Buy now</u> Mr Customer, I'm sure you can <u>see the benefits of this proposal</u>, can't you? A <u>buy product</u> of this arrangement is the free service support. <u>Buy</u> the way, we can arrange delivery next week, if <u>you go ahead right now</u>."

Please spend some time to work out how you can use embedded suggestions in your every day communication with customers, as they are very influential.

Let Me Quote You On That!

Using quotes is a very subtle way of indirect influence. The quote language pattern is very easy to use - just take the thing you'd like to say to the customer and put it into quotes!

Your customer will have little, if any, awareness of you using different levels of communication. They may not notice at a conscious level but the suggestions you make will register at an unconscious level! Putting a suggestion in quotes sneaks it by the conscious reasoning and gets it processed at an unconscious level.

When I first learned about quotes I was told, "Quotes are very powerful tools of influence." and, "You should use quotes to get people to say yes to your suggestions." I was also told that, "You can be really blatant about using quotes and people won't even notice."

Perhaps you can see in the above paragraph how I have been using quotes to influence you to use quotes!

A powerful use of quotes is to quote a satisfied customer or client and use this to make your suggestion to your customer. For example, "Fred Jones at ABC company told me that *'This is the best product available'*"

You didn't say that your product is the best available, *Fred Jones* did!

I am sure that you can see how you can embed suggestions within quotes and weave them into your sales presentation, can't you? Oh and as my NLP trainer said to me, "Use tag questions, embedded commands, phonological ambiguities and quotes as much as possible because they are incredibly influential."

Time for the next chapter, isn't it?

The Second Pivot Point

Step 8 of the Bare Knuckle Selling process: "Reinforce Needs, Criteria and Solutions"

As with Step Six of the Bare Knuckle Selling process ("Agreement to Proceed"), this is a small section of the sales call. Again, like Step Six, it is a very important and often overlooked part of the selling process.

This step of the sales call reviews and reinforces the following steps with the customer:

- Step 4: Understand customer needs and criteria
- Step 5: Understand the customer's budget
- Step 6: Get the agreement to proceed
- Step 7: Propose and Present

As the sales call with the customer may have taken some time and will have covered a lot of ground, this step serves to remind the customer of what has been said and what they've agreed to so far. As a result it tees the customer up very nicely for you to close the sale.

An example of what to say would be:

"Mr Customer, can I just summarise what we have discussed so far? My understanding is that you are concerned about (problem) and the effects it is having on your business. We also discussed that you are worried about the longer term affect that (problem) will have on profitability. That's right, isn't it? Due to the predicted financial impact of (problem) you are able to invest up to £10,000 to get this problem solved. That's correct, isn't it? You also said that you needed a supplier who was 'flexible' and would 'tailor' their service to your specific requirements. You agreed that if I could show you a way to address this issue and show you how you would benefit, you would be interested, didn't you? I showed you that our service would benefit you by (benefit, benefit, benefit, benefit) and how our particular strengths are how 'flexible' we are in our ability to 'tailor' our service to the very specific needs that you have. Does that cover all your points?"

As you are running through your summary you need to pay full and complete attention to the customer. You can imagine yourself as a coiled cobra waiting for the exact moment to strike, you need to watch for the customer telling you it is time to close the sale! And that, my selling cobras, is the subject of the next chapter!

Securing The Result That You & Your Customer Want

Step 9 of the Bare Knuckle Selling process: "Secure the Result"

If you ask any sales manager to detail what he looks for in an ideal salesperson they will usually state that they want 'strong closers'. Closing, or securing the result, is an essential part of selling. Closing is getting the customer to say "Yes" to your proposal, to say "Yes" to spending money with you. If you can't close sales then you aren't selling – you are just having a conversation!

People sometimes ask me if it is really necessary to close. If you have done a really good job of understanding the customer's needs and criteria, and have done a great job of presenting your proposal, is closing really necessary? Won't the customer just volunteer an order?

Well, perhaps in some cases they might but a comprehensive survey by The Institute of Purchasing Management involving people who are professional buyers (purchasing managers, production managers, office managers, directors etc) established that *only one in five customers will ever volunteer an order!*

The other four (or 80% of all buyers) expect the salesperson to ask for the order, or put another way   to close the sale. So sales people who don't ask for the order and are waiting for the customer to volunteer to buy are missing out on 80% of their potential sales.

For a Bare Knuckle Seller, who after reading this chapter is a master closer of sales, that is great news! That gives us far more business to grab at the expense of the less able sales people out there.

One of the reasons that some sales people feel that they shouldn't close sales (and for my money if you are in sales and you don't attempt to close sales then you really ought to find a different profession) is that they feel that closing is in some way 'high pressure' and unethical.

If you have followed the Bare Knuckle Selling process through so far then you will have established the customer's needs and criteria and demonstrated how your product or service will solve his problems, take away his pain and make him a happier person!

You will have established if the customer really needs your product or service. If he does then what could be unethical about encouraging the customer to go ahead?

People procrastinate. They put off doing things even when they know they should. Perhaps you have done this in the past? Customers are just the same. Sometimes they need some encouragement to do what is right for them. If your product or service can really help a customer solve their problems and can help them get what they want, then I would go so far as to say that you are morally obligated to encourage the customer to go ahead! So not closing in this case would be unethical.

And to be somewhat selfish for a moment, if you have identified a genuine customer need and you don't get the order, then you can bet your bottom dollar that at some stage one of your competitors will!

When I was a sales manager I once had the privilege of managing a very successful young lady, Louisa, who was one of my best sales people. Louisa was very good at the entire sales process but her strongest ability was in closing the sale. She was the best closer in my team. I was very interested to know why and explored this with her.

She explained that when working for a previous company she had been selling water coolers. She would cold call on offices, banks, shops, factories and warehouses to sell them water coolers. The object of the sale was to get the customers to agree to have a water cooler (or water coolers) sited in their premises and to buy the containers of water that they needed on an on going basis. Louisa explained to me that the water cooler market was, like most other industries, very competitive and that if you wanted to be a success in selling them you had to get good at closing. If you didn't close the sale, if the customer wanted to 'think about it', then you stood a very good chance that you would subsequently find out that another company had installed a water cooler into the customer's premises. Louisa told me that, fundamentally water coolers are water coolers. They all dispense cold water and there is not a lot to choose between them! Once she had succeeded in getting an appointment with the decision maker she had to get very good at closing the sale so she did not miss out.

I don't think that it is much different for many products and services. Although I highly recommend that you understand and sell what is unique about your product or service, often you will be selling in a competitive field with many high quality competitors. If you don't close the sale and get the business when the chance is there then you can be assured that one of your competitors will be quite happy to do so.

Finishing Moves

An important thing is to understand when it is a good time to close a sale. My simple answer is: whenever a customer is ready to buy!

To successfully close a sale the customer must:

- Need your product or service
- Want your product or service
- Be able to use your product or service
- Be able to afford your product or service

If these factors are in place, and they should be if you have followed the Bare Knuckle Selling process correctly so far, it is time to close.

From many years of experience as a sales manager accompanying sales professionals into thousands of calls and running countless sales training programmes with sales people doing selling role plays on camera, one of the most common pieces of feedback is that they could have closed the sale much earlier than they did.

As soon as the customer signals to you that they are ready to buy you must close the sale. Carrying on selling past this point can actually result in lost sales.

I remember a time when I was manning a stand at a trade exhibition. A gentleman walked up onto my stand and said that although he wasn't going to buy anything today he was interested to understand more about one of my company's products. I took him over to a desk on our stand and we sat down. Although he had already expressed some interest, I asked him a series of questions to understand his needs, problems and criteria. Then I asked some questions to clarify his budget, summarised our conversation to date and asked him if he wanted to spend fifteen minutes while I talked to him about the product in question. He agreed to this and I opened up my sales presenter which had a large colour picture of the product in it. Before I had a chance to say a word, the gentleman looked at the picture and said, "I'll take it!"

As I already understood his needs and knew that our product would be appropriate, I closed the sales presenter, reached for my order pad and took the order! If I had carried on selling, the moment (and the order) may have been lost.

Although it is rare for a customer to respond like this, it does happen and it is important to close the order whenever the customer is ready to buy. This is known as the ABC principle.

The ABC Principle

ABC stands for Always Be Closing. Always be prepared and ready to close, anytime the customer indicates to you that they are ready to buy. So how do you know when the customer is ready to buy? The customer will tell you. They will send you very clear verbal and non verbal signals that they are ready to buy.

Buying Signals

Buying signals are verbal or non verbal indications that the customer is ready to buy. These can occur at any time in the selling process and when you see or hear them it is a good opportunity to close. A buying signal is a noticeable change in voice, posture, attitude or behaviour and can indicate that a buying decision is near. Buying signals include:

Nodding Agreement

Nodding of the head is often an unconscious action that usually indicates that the customer is responding favourably to what you are saying. Nodding can and does occur during any stage of the sale but is particularly important when it occurs during the 'Reinforce Needs, Criteria and Solutions' step. If you recall, this is when you are summarising your conversation and presentation. Several nods at this stage indicate it is time to go for a close!

Verbally Accepting

As with nodding, a number of, "Yes", "Uh huh", "Right", "Yep", "Okay", or similar verbal responses is a good sign. It is not uncommon for nodding and verbally accepting to be done together.

Leaning Forwards

If the customer suddenly leans forward, towards the product on show or towards the proposal on their desk, this can be a powerful buying signal. Non verbally they are telling you that they want to take a closer look.

Brighten Up

If the customer suddenly brightens up, and their energy lifts this is often a sign that they have emotionally bought into your proposal.

Talking Faster

Many people have a tendency to speak faster when they get excited about something. If your customer starts to talk more quickly then this is usually a good sign!

Touching The Product/Proposal

Another buying signal can be when the customer moves to pick up the product being sold, or picks up the proposal. This is a sign of interest/owenership.

Making Notes

If the customer takes their pen or pencil and makes notes on a piece of paper or on their copy of your proposal then this can also be a buying signal.

I was once leading a multi million pound negotiation (if you want to know more about how to negotiate killer deals then read my book *Bare Knuckle Negotiation*) with a particularly aggressive and demanding customer.

Our negotiation team had spent about two hours locked into a very tense negotiation with the customer's negotiation team. The key point of the negotiation was that the customer wanted a price discount as they had doubled their business with me inside eighteen months. I wanted to list two more of our products with the customer. It was in my interest to give the customer the discount they wanted as, due to the volume they were now purchasing, I had to remain competitive or they may have been tempted to look elsewhere.

Although I did need to ensure their purchasing price was competitive, there was an opportunity to gain significantly at the same time. I knew that due to their scale that the profit I would make from two additional product listings would far outweigh the cost of increasing their discount on the existing product!

I was therefore holding out on increasing their discount, unless they agreed to take two additional products. I had proposed a rather bold listing of four new products with the realistic intention of listing two of them.

The buying director had a copy of my proposal in front of him that contained the specifications and pricing of the new products. During a pause in the proceedings, he leant forward, picked up his pencil and circled two of the products.

I said, "Tim, if you list Product B and Product C (the two products that he had circled) as from next month and commit to an initial order of one container per product then I will take a look at your discount on Product A." Then I shut up and looked at him.

After a moment or two of silence he said, "Okay, let's go ahead." He then reached over to shake my hand and we sorted out the finer details of the new deal.

I had read the combination of leaning forwards and circling the two products with his pencil as a buying signal and I moved to close the deal. Although selling and negotiation are different, as we will explore later, the principle of buying signals still applies.

Calculating Numbers

If a customer starts to use their calculator to consider some costs or write costs down then this can be a sign that they are considering proceeding.

Raising Concerns

Another buying signal that is often misinterpreted as a problem by some sales people is where the customer starts to raise concerns about the product or service. We will go into much greater detail in this chapter about how to handle these, but for now, I would like to consider them as a positive sign.

When a customer raises concerns, I often view it that they are really considering buying the product or service, and as they are thinking about it, some concerns may arise such as the price or "what if it breaks down?" or "what if I haven't got room?" These kind of questions often suggest that the customer has already 'mentally bought' and is now just considering the practicalities.

So as you are proceeding through the sale, you need to be like the cobra mentioned earlier, poised and ready to strike at the first sign of a buying signal! Now let's take a look at a variety of closing methods that you can use.

Revealed   The Master Closing Method of The World's Greatest Sales people!

Wow! How is that for a promise? The master closing method of the world's greatest sales people! Sounds exciting, doesn't it? When I am running my sales training programmes I tell the participants that I am going to reveal this secret to them.

I then tell them that before I do, I am going to ask them to participate in a small experiment. I give each of them an envelope and ask them to put a sum of money (they get to choose how much) in it and to write the amount and their name on the front of the envelope. I then ask them to give the envelopes to me. Without fail, everyone complies and hands the money to me.

I then tell them that this is the master closing method of the world's greatest sales people – *they just ask*. Yes, that's it – *they simply ask for the order*. I go on to point out that I asked them to put their hard earned cash into an envelope and give it to me. I didn't tell them why, I simply asked them and they all complied with my request! They usually then ask me if they will get their money back... but that's a different story!

Most of the time closing the sale is as simple as that – you just have to ask. So why do so many sales people fail to close the sale? One of the reasons is that they are scared of the rejection if the customer says "No".

I have made thousands of sales closes in my career and I am pleased to report that not one of them has resulted in any form of physical injury! Nobody (to the best of my knowledge) has been physically attacked, maimed, wounded or killed as a result of attempting to close a sale!

The fear is an illusion. It is just a fear of rejection. As soon as you conquer that fear your closing ability improves. I was very fortunate to begin my sales career with a job that involved lots of door to door cold calling on people in their homes. It doesn't take long doing that job before you get pretty immune to being rejected!

If you have followed the Bare Knuckle Selling process correctly, you will already have a very good idea that the customer wants to proceed anyway. However, if for some reason they don't, can't or won't proceed at least by attempting to close you will find this out and can swiftly move onto the next customer.

Close Sales The Same Way That You Get Into Your Bath!

In order for me to feel confident before making my final close in a sale, I use a process that gives me indications throughout the sale that I am on the right track with the customer, and that they are likely to say "yes" to going ahead.

When you have a bath it is very rare that after running the water you jump straight in! What you will do is to test the temperature with your hand first. If this feels good you will then proceed to dipping your toe in the water. If this feels good then you get into the bath.

You can use the same method to gently close sales in a way that is effective and respectful of the customer. You can use the following process:

1. Ask testing questions
2. Ask trial closing questions
3. Ask final closing questions

Testing Questions

Testing questions are used when making your presentation to the customer. It is useful that after stating a benefit of your product or service you ask:

"How do you feel about that?" or

"Is that important to you?" or

"Does this make sense to you so far?"

and after your presentation

"Does that cover all the points we discussed?"

Note the customer's reactions. If you get a number of positive responses (or buying signals) during your presentation and summary then move to a trial closing question.

Trial Closing Questions

With trial closing questions you are not asking, "Will you buy?" but rather, "Will you buy if I ask you to?" Examples of trial closing questions include:

"If we could do that would you be interested?"

"Can you see how this does everything you want?"

"Is this what you were looking for?"

"Would this be what you had in mind?"

"If we were to assume that you are going ahead where would you be siting it?"

"If we can get the specification you require, how close are you to going ahead?"

Trial closes can be very useful to flush out any problems, concerns or hesitations that the customer may have. We will be looking at how to deal with those later.

After getting a positive response to two or three trial closes you then need to move to a final closing question.

Final Closing Question

This is when you take the customer's order or get their agreement to proceed. As mentioned earlier, I favour the direct approach, or as it is sometimes called the assumptive approach, where you confidently assume the sale will go ahead. I must stress that I only use this approach when I am confident that I fully understand the customer's needs and criteria and have received a series of positive responses and buying signals.

Here are a few phrases I like to use when asking the customer for their order:

"Would you like to go ahead now?"

"Would you like to try it?"

"Shall we get the paperwork done then?"

"Shall we get started right away?"

These are nice, soft and conversational closes that are very effective. I very rarely use anything else, although I will detail later in this chapter a number of other closing methods for you to consider.

Other final closing questions are:

"So, when do you want delivery?"

"Shall we get started right away?"

"Shall we get a date in the diary?"

"So are we going ahead then?"

This three stage process to closing the sale is very effective but it does rely upon you asking the customer for their agreement to go ahead! The secret of closing is basically asking. Ask, ask, ask! Never leave a sales presentation without having asked for the order. In addition, as we shall see later, you may have to ask several times.

Shut Up!

It is very important that when you have made an attempt to close the sale that you remain silent. After you have said, "So would you like to try it?" shut up! Just shut up. Resist the urge to speak. The silence prompts the customer into responding. The silence creates a vacuum that sucks a response from the customer into it. Some people take quite some time before responding, so don't lose your nerve and speak. The golden rule is:

When you have closed - SHUT UP!

There is a fine line between persistence and pestering. I would urge you to err on the side of pestering! I think it is better to run the risk of overdoing your close than it is to miss your opportunity to close the sale entirely.

Other Closing Methods

Now that you understand that closing is really about asking the customer for their agreement to go ahead, we can now take a look at some different closing techniques.

A word of caution at this stage: some of these techniques are rather well known, particularly by professional buyers, and as a result need to be used subtly and with care. If someone suspects they're having a 'technique' used on them it can do a lot of damage to your hard earned rapport. But, when they are used skilfully, and at the appropriate time, they are very powerful. When a customer is closed by a Bare Knuckle Selling master they won't even notice!

Every one of these techniques has been road tested and proved effective by yours truly and countless other sales professionals.

The Alternative Close

Although this is one of the oldest closes in the book and if used poorly is a very obvious sales tactic, I have found that if used with care it can be very effective. The alternative close uses a choice the customer has to make as a close. For example:

"Do you want delivery this week or next week?"

"Will you want the basic model or the upgraded model?"

"Do you want to pay by credit card or cash?"

I have used this close in some very sophisticated, high ticket sales and if used with care it works a treat.

The Order Form Close

If you use any type of order form or paperwork (or if you can invent some so that you can use this close) then you might like to try this technique.

With this close you simply start completing the customer's order as you are speaking to them. If you ask, "What is the exact spelling of your last name?" and they tell you without hesitation, then you can be almost 100% certain that the sale is closed.

The Procrastination Close

This is a more risky closing method and should be kept for times when, after having made several attempts to close, or indeed sales calls to the customer, you get the sense that they are procrastinating. It is a 'high pressure' close that either closes the sale or lets you know not to waste any more time on the customer in question. This is only for the very brave Bare Knuckle Seller! Here is how it works:

"Mr Customer, either this is a good idea and you should go ahead or it is not a good idea and you ought to forget it. But one way or another why don't we make a decision right now so I can stop taking up your time on these visits."

Then slide your completed contract or order form across the desk to the customer. Put a tick mark next to where the customer needs to sign, put your pen down on top of the paperwork, remain silent and wait for the customer to do or say something! In my experience approximately 6 times out of 10 the customer signs the order.

On the subject of signing paperwork, always put a tick by where the customer needs to sign and not a cross. People associate crosses with getting things wrong at school, whereas ticks are for when you get things right! Unconsciously the use of a tick sends another positive message.

It is also advisable to avoid using words such as, "signing the contract" as this can conjure up thoughts of legal contracts with all of their attendant penalty clauses and expensive legal advisors!

It is far better to refer to, "OK ing the agreement" as this sounds positive or the more cheeky and light hearted, "Can I have your autograph!"

The Normal Close

This close uses the Social Proof principle of Robert Cialdini. To use this you say:

"In the situation our customers *normally* order the X model"

or

"In our experience sales managers (or whatever category of person you are selling to) *normally* choose the..."

You then say, "I guess you want to do likewise?"

If it is normal then everyone must be doing it, right?

The Similar Situation Close

This is a slight variation on the normal close. Here you relate a situation similar to your customer and let them realise it could have similar consequences or benefits. For example:

"You know... about a month ago I had a client facing a decision very similar to the one we are discussing. He decided to install the equipment and when I called to see him last week he was already saving time and money!"

or

"You know... about two months ago I had a client facing a similar decision to the one you are facing. He decided to sign up for the private medical insurance and within just a couple of weeks he had need for it."

The Puppy Dog Close

This close is based upon the story of a pet shop owner who had some potential customers who just couldn't decide whether to buy a puppy as a pet. The wily pet shop owner invited them to take the puppy home for the weekend to, "see how they got on". After the weekend the customer's children had fallen in love with the puppy and the sale was closed.

This principle is used extensively with various companies offering free trials of their equipment or service. The free trial reduces the concerns the customer may have about making a mistake and, by the time the free trial concludes, the customer will have benefited from the product or service and will be now reluctant to do without it.

The Three Question Close

This close uses a combination of three questions to close the sale. For example:

"Can you see where this equipment will save you money?"

"Are you interested in saving money?"

(Best said in a light hearted or humorous way to avoid this question sounding patronising)

"When do you want to start saving money?"

To which the customer usually says, "As soon as possible!" to which you reply, "So let's get the agreement sorted out then!"

The Ascending Close

This close is a variation on the three question close and asks a series of questions that each get a "yes". This establishes a pattern that hypnotists refer to as a 'yes set'. It establishes a pattern of agreement that the customer follows, for example:

Salesperson: *"So we have identified that your needs are X, Y and Z. That's right, isn't it?"*

Customer: "Yes"

Salesperson: *"And it's very important to you that your suppliers are able to do A. B and C"*

Customer: "Yes"

Salesperson: *"And I've shown you how this product will enable you to satisfy need X haven't I?"*

Customer: "Yes"

Salesperson: *"And we've also seen how it meets needs Y and Z also, haven't we?"*

Customer "Yes"

Salesperson: *"And you now know that as a supplier our strengths are being able to do A. B and C for our clients, don't you?"*

Customer: "Yes"

Salesperson: *"So shall we go ahead?"*

Customer: "Yes!"

You will be able to see how the pattern of questions, not only elicit a "yes" each time but also reinforce how the benefits of the product or service in question meet the customer's identified needs and criteria. Highly influential stuff!

The Half Nelson Close

This close is named after a wrestling hold. While I am not an advocate of fighting with customers it is a very useful way to close a sale!

It is used when a customer asks a question about the product or service which you then use to close the sale. For example:

Customer: "Does it come with a full years warranty?"

Salesperson: *"If I can arrange that warranty do you want to go ahead?"*

or

Customer: "Does it come with a display stand?"

Salesperson: *"If I can arrange a display stand do you want to go ahead?"*

So there you have it, a veritable armoury of powerful closing techniques! Please take some time to determine which ones work for you and practice them until they feel natural. Then get closing!

Give Them A Reason To Act Now

As procrastinating is something that many people do and indeed don't want to do, it is always recommended to give the customer a really good reason to act immediately. If you don't do this then there is a good chance that the sale will drift. The customer will get wrapped up in all of the other things they have to do and then forget all about your product or service – at least for the time being.

Give the customer a reason to act now. At this stage you will know if your product or service will help the customer, if it will solve their problems, alleviate their pain and help them to get what they want. So, it would be wrong of you not to strongly encourage them to make the correct decision and go ahead right now!

An effective way to get them to act is to revisit the problems and pain that the customer has. Remind them of that pain and then demonstrate how the longer they delay the worse it will get.

For example, if you can show the customer that you can save them money on, say their printing requirements, then each week that they continue to use their current supplier they are quite literally throwing money away.

You can use emotive language and describe it as though the customer is putting a pile of ten pound notes on their table and setting fire to them every week! This rather dramatic example has proved an effective illustration on a number of occasions for me.

If you have limited stock availability or service capability then you can use this 'scarcity' to encourage the customer to act before someone else does. While I am not a big fan of the rather obvious, "You must place your order now because the sale ends on Friday!" approach, if you do have a genuine shortage or limited time offer then use it.

Professor Robert Cialdini discovered that people are motivated to say "Yes" to a proposal if the item in question is perceived to be scarce. He also discovered that items that are scarce are perceived to be more valuable than items that are more readily available. Providing this concept is not overused it is very effective at motivating the customer to take action.

How Many Closes Does It Take To Finally Close A Sale?

While many times it will take just one close to secure the business, research and personal experience suggests that 80% of sales are closed after the 5th closing attempt.

That is why the ABC rule – Always Be Closing – is so important. Pursue the close with persistence and keep on closing until the customer says "Yes!"

Handling Customer Concerns

Sometimes in a sale, a customer may express a concern about your product or service. Some sales people and sales trainers refer to these as 'objections'. I do not favour this description as it implies that the salesperson and the customer are engaged in some sort of confrontational process. For this reason I prefer to refer to them merely as 'concerns'.

A concern is where the customer indicates that they have some worry, reluctance or some other issue preventing them from going ahead with the sale. There are three broad categories of concern:

1. A red herring

Sometimes customers will offer up concerns that aren't really concerns at all. They are just something that the customer throws at you. They may do this to feel that they are giving you a hard time and as a result will get a better deal. Or they may throw a red herring concern at you as they are thinking out loud about your proposal. I have seen many occasions where a customer will express a concern only to retract it a few seconds later after they have considered what they have said!

It is also worth considering that professional buyers will sometimes fire a lot of red herring concerns at a salesperson to put them on the back foot. This is often done as a precursor to attempting to drive down the price.

2. A misunderstanding

This category of concern is where the customer has not understood some aspect of your proposal, product or service correctly. Sometimes this will be because they have not listened properly, or it is a complicated product or service Other times the misunderstanding could be down to the fact that you have not explained your proposal in sufficient detail or with enough clarity yet.

3. A genuine concern

This category of concern is where the customer has a real and genuine reason that is stopping then from going ahead.

In a moment we will take a good look at how to deal with all three categories of concern.

When To Handle Concerns

There are four times that you can handle customer concerns:

1. Before your presentation
2. During your presentation
3. After your presentation
4. Never! This would be reserved for red herring concerns, which can often be gently ignored.

Inoculating Against Concerns

If you are taking a holiday to an exotic and tropical location the common wisdom is to visit your doctor to get inoculated against various illnesses and diseases before you go. You don't wait to catch yellow fever or typhoid so you get your jabs.

In the same way, you can inoculate your sales presentation from some concerns both before and during your presentation. Most sales people can tell you the concerns that customers express most frequently about their products and services. If specific concerns are raised fairly frequently it can be effective to nail these either before or during your presentation.

There are two ways to do this:

"Don't Make The Same Mistake"

People don't like to make mistakes and they don't like to look stupid. The fear of making mistakes and looking stupid can be one of the reasons that customers don't want to proceed with purchasing. We can use this same motivation factor to kill off specific concerns both before and during the sales presentation.

Let us assume that a number of your customers have expressed a concern that your new cutting edge product is complicated and therefore difficult to operate. You can inoculate against this by saying:

"Mr Customer, some people make the mistake of thinking that because our product is so cutting edge that it is complicated and difficult to operate. What they find is that in fact its new control panel makes it really simple to understand and use."

Nobody wants to make a mistake do they? So our customer, who does not want to make a mistake, will immediately decide that your product is simple to understand and use!

Another variation upon this is, "Mr Customer, some of our most satisfied customers initially made the mistake of thinking that our new cutting edge product must be complicated and difficult to operate. What they have found is that in fact its new control panel makes it simple to understand and use."

"Don't Be A Whiner!"

There is something about a whinging and whining voice that people really dislike. Remember the last time you heard a small child (or even a fully grown adult) use that whining tone of voice. Its effect is similar to fingernails being dragged down a blackboard. Cuts right through you, doesn't it?

You can use this fact to great effect to inoculate against concerns. Using the same example as previously, here is how this technique works:

"Mr Customer, when some people hear that our product is cutting edge they say (Now use your very best whiny voice for the next sentence), *'It's so complicated and difficult to operate!'* even though it's not."

The vast majority of people have such a dislike of a whining tone of voice that they will instantly move away from ever having had such a concern about your product themselves. They don't want to be associated with that horrible, whiny voice!

Inoculating against concerns is a very powerful way of making sure that commonly expressed concerns are killed off deader than a Dodo before and during your presentation.

Take some of the concerns that customers in your industry bring up most commonly and devise some ways to inoculate against them. Remember that you can use them before you make your presentation and during it when discussing particular elements of your proposal.

Handling Concerns When They Are Raised By The Customer

There are a number of ways to deal with concerns expressed by customers. The first important point is that you mustn't panic. It is quite rare for a sale to go through to completion without the customer expressing at least one concern!

The fact that a customer has raised a concern does not mean that they are not going to go ahead. Relax... it's all part of the selling game!

Professional sellers understand that customers raising concerns is just part of the selling process and they are prepared to handle them with persistence. This puts them into a different league than most.

A piece of international research into the reaction of sales people to customer concerns revealed that:

- 44% of sales people gave up after receiving the first customer concern

- 22% of sales people gave up after receiving the second customer concern

- 16% of sales people gave up after receiving the third customer concern

- 10% of sales people gave up after receiving the fourth customer concern

This leaves just 8% of the sales people still selling after the fourth concern.

The other startling conclusion from the survey is that 73% of the customers voiced *five or more concerns before being sure enough to place an order!*

Combine the figures together and the research tells us that:

Just 8% of the sales people will win
73% of the business that's available.

It is therefore vital that unless you want to join the ranks of the 'sales no hopers' that you need to get really superb at welcoming and handling customer concerns. Being able to do this will place you into the top few percent of all of the best sales people in the world.

Bare Knuckle Sellers enjoy eating customer concerns for breakfast!

I view customers expressing concerns as a good sign. They can mean that the customer is really starting to think about going ahead is starting to consider the practicalities involved.

Or they can indicate that there is some aspect of the product or service that the customer is seeking more information about. You can reframe all expressed concerns as being requests for further information. The customer is looking to you, the salesperson to answer this request.

The Initial Response

How you initially respond to the customer's concern is important. You want to appear calm, professional and unruffled but also grateful and even delighted that they raised the concern. For example, after hearing the customer express a concern say:

"That's a good point. I'm glad you brought that up."

"That's an important point and it's the initial reaction of some of our best customers."

"I'm really glad you raised that point Mr Customer."

Once you have initially responded in this manner you can then move onto handling the concern in a variety of ways...

Drill Further Into The Concern

It is often necessary to drill further down into a concern to understand it more fully.

You can ask, "I'm sure you've got a good reason for raising that concern. Can I ask what it is?"

This will result in the customer expanding upon what lies behind the expressed concern so that you can deal with it more effectively.

Feel, Felt, Found

This is my favourite method for handling customer's concerns. I have found it to be simple, elegant and effective. If I am selling my services as a sales trainer and a customer was to express concern over spending a large amount of money (I don't come cheap) due to the fact that they have such a large sales force to be trained I could respond:

"Mr Customer that's an important point and I'm glad you brought it up, I understand exactly how you <u>feel</u>. A number of my clients with large sales forces <u>felt</u> exactly the same way, until they <u>found</u> that my sales training delivered an exceptional return on investment with increases in sales of between 10 and 20%!"

You can adapt this very elegant technique to any product or service. If you were selling photocopiers and the customer expressed a concern that the machine you were recommending had more functions than the customer needed you could say:

"Mr Customer, that's a good point. I'm glad you brought it up. I understand exactly how you <u>feel</u>. Many of my clients who are now using this very machine <u>felt</u> exactly the same way, until they <u>found</u> that once they had the machine installed they were able to use it in so many more useful ways than they previously thought of, and ended up saving even more time and money than they had anticipated!"

Feel, felt, found has a very clever structure:

- Feel – empathises with the customer and acknowledges his concern in a respectful way.

- Felt – linguistically moves the concern into the past tense; it is no longer valid and uses the power of testimonial and social proof.

- Found – allows you to reinforce the benefits of your product and service once again.

This is a very effective way to handle customers concerns.

Restate, Isolate, Classify

This is another simple process that you can follow to handle customer's concerns.

Let's use the example of a customer in a retail business that has a concern that he just does not have the space in his shop for your new product and its display stand.

Restate:

"Mr Customer that is a good point. If I understand you correctly you are saying that you don't think that you can find the space for this new display stand?"

This demonstrates to the customer that you have been listening and are treating his concerns respectfully.

Isolate:

"Is that the only reason you are concerned about going ahead?"

or

"Is this the only question we need to address for you to say 'yes' to going ahead?"

This isolates the concern and also helps you uncover if it is a genuine concern ("Yes, you can see how crowded the shop floor is looking.") or if it is just a red herring ("No, its more that I already have several products listed in that category!") It will also bring out any additional concerns if there are any.

You can then use a process called 'If/Suppose' to further clarify the concern:

"If I could show you how we can find some space could we go ahead?"

or

"Suppose we could find some space?"

Classify:

Dependant upon the customer responses so far, you will now be able to classify the concern as a red herring, misunderstanding or genuine.

The appropriate action for different classifications of concern is:

Red Herring:

Tactfully ignore. If the customer has said, "Well the real reason is..." focus upon the real reason and leave the red herring to wither and die!

Misunderstanding:

Apologise for the misunderstanding. "Mr Customer, sorry for causing confusion, that's my fault for not explaining correctly. The new display stand is actually wall mounted not free standing so floor space won't be an issue, will it?"

Genuine:

For genuine concerns we use a technique known as the 'see saw'. I am sure that as a child you will have played on a see saw (or teeter totter as they are also known). You may have had the experience of sitting high in the air on one end of a see saw while a much older (and larger) child sat on the other end.

We can think about the customer's concern as a large child sitting on one end of the see saw. We need to counter balance the concern. We do this by piling benefits onto the other end of the see saw to outweigh the concern.

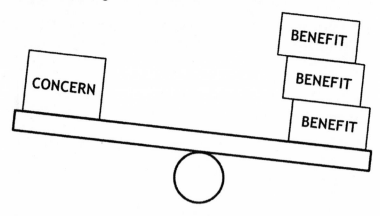

For example, the customer may genuinely be short of room to site your display stand. The benefits of the customer going to the trouble of finding space in his shop to site your stand could include:

- New innovative product with a higher retail price will add to the value of the category it is part of

- The new product commands a higher retail selling price than several products it is designed to replace which means more cash in the retailer's till and less hassle

- The new product allows the retailer to make a higher percentage profit per unit sold

- The display stand features through the line details of your new multi million pound TV campaign which will increase customer pick up of the product

- The new display stand has a greater capacity and needs less stock replenishment which means less labour cost and hassle

- Due to its innovative design, the new display stand can be sited in key traffic areas in the store increasing consumer sales of the product

- The new display stand can be sited near the shop tills to maximise impulse purchase

- Retailers who utilise the display stand qualify for a one off discount on initial stocks purchased

Phew! With some, or all, of these benefits stacked on the other end of your see saw you stand a good chance that the customer will feel very motivated to find the space for your display stand.

This principle, of making the benefits of going ahead outweigh the cost or inconvenience of going ahead, will satisfy many concerns. It demonstrates a strong case for the benefits of the customer going ahead. Show the customer that the benefits outweigh the costs and you will satisfy their concerns and motivate them to action.

Further Concern Handling Methods

Here are a few more powerful concern handling methods to add to your Bare Knuckle Selling armoury:

Turn The Objection Into A Question

With this technique you simply treat the concern as a question. For example,

Customer: "This seems very complicated and far too advanced for us."

Salesperson: "So what you are asking me Mr Customer if I understand you correctly is why do our units have such an extensive range of advanced features?"

You would then move onto selling the features and benefits of your product or service again.

Turn The Objection Into A Reason To Go Ahead

With this technique you flip the concern into the very reason why your customer should buy. Taking the previous example again:

Customer: "This seems very complicated and far too advanced for us."

Salesperson: "Mr Customer that is exactly the reason we do so much business! Once clients have installed our units they tell us that they are blown away with how powerfully the unit helps them to (insert features and benefits that are related to the customers needs and criteria that you identified earlier in the selling process.)

"I Want To Think It Over"

Sometimes, perhaps with big ticket purchases, customers really do want to compare and contrast the various options that they have received. A situation where a customer has invited a number of suppliers in to tender for a particular piece of business will often involve the customer considering the various bids received.

However, in many cases, when a customers says, "I want to think it over" what they are actually telling you is that you haven't convinced them yet!

A good response to, "I want to think it over" is, "Mr Customer what specific aspect of the proposal aren't you sure about yet?" or "Mr Customer, what aspect of my proposal aren't you satisfied on yet?"

This approach will usually flush out if there is an area that you need to do some more work on. Please note the use of the, "aren't you sure of yet." The use of the 'yet' pre supposes that the customer will be satisfied in the future!

On many occasions I have experienced the customer responding to, "What aspect of my proposal aren't you satisfied on yet?" with "Err... nothing really, okay let's go ahead!"

Please remember that one of the biggest challenges a salesperson faces is people's tendency to procrastinate. By continuing to pursue the sale despite the fact they said, "I want to think about it" you can overcome this procrastination.

How To Handle Customers Concerns About Price

One of the things I am most frequently asked about when training sales people is how to handle customers who want to drive the price down. Sales people are only too used to having the price gun put to their head.

They are only too used to the threat: "If you don't drop your price then you will walk out without an order."

One of the reasons that the Bare Knuckle Selling process includes understanding the customer's budget early on in the sales process is to help with just this scenario. Understanding the customer's budget helps enormously with price concerns.

However you may still come across them and understandably it can be very tempting to shave a few percent off your price to secure the order. However, you don't always need to do this. As a Bare Knuckle Seller you will sell more and at a higher price. Let's take a look at how.

Reality Check

Before we delve into this area, let's do a reality check. The evidence would suggest that business gets progressively more competitive, with companies often competing with each other on price.

The consumer is getting better informed and through the internet can search for the most competitive price on many items.

It is good business sense to ensure that your product or service is correctly priced for your market place. However, correctly priced does not necessarily mean cheap.

You do not always need to be the cheapest to get the business. There are always factors other than just the price of the product to consider – reliability, quality, convenience, suitability to name just a few. So, despite what a customer might say, it is very rarely just about price.

The Customer Does Not Want The Cheapest

Regardless what the customer will say to you they rarely just want to buy the cheapest product or service. What they *do* want is to ensure that they get value for money. That is a very different situation to wanting things cheap.

Truly cheap items are often just that – cheap. They may lack quality, be out of date, and be manufactured from lower grade components or inferior ingredients.

I am firmly of the opinion that people are very happy to pay good money for things that meet their needs, solve their problems, ease their pain and make them feel good.

You only have to look at the huge trade in luxury goods to know that price isn't everything! I'm something of a living example. I drive a Mercedes and wear Armani suits. Neither of these things are cheap items to purchase are they? However, they are both high quality and high value for money products.

There is more money, wealth and prosperity in our society than there ever has been before. Yes, business can be competitive, but it does not mean that you have to cut your margins to the bone to survive.

I am not aware of any company that is a market leader in its industry that is the cheapest on everything they sell. They provide quality products and services that meet people's needs. People are happy to pay.

Having said that, the modern customer is likely to be very demanding on price! If possible they want high quality *and* low cost. As this is not economically possible for most businesses, let's look at how you can handle your customer's requests for price reductions and discounts!

Don't Blame Them - It's Good Business Practice

You can hardly blame a customer for driving a hard bargain can you? Any money saved is money in the bank for extra profits.

I drive very, very hard bargains. I sell hard and I negotiate hard too. So I cannot blame one of my customers for doing likewise can I? I work very hard to secure value for money for myself and so will your customers.

Make Sure You Have Defined The Difference

When a customer tells you that they have received a lower price offer from a competitor, make sure you understand what the customer means. They may have told you that they can get the same (or a similar) product from your competitor for a 'big discount'.

What on earth does 'a big discount' mean? It could mean any amount! It could mean a discount of £10, £100, £1000, £10,000, £100,000 or even more!

Or it could be a percentage discount rather than a cash discount. It is vital to understand what you are talking about. If the service or item being sold is a regular purchase is the discount a one off discount or is it on going?

Does the customer get the discount up front or does it get paid only after remaining loyal to the supplier for a fixed amount of time, or in return for achieving a specific sales volume?

You must understand the specifics. As you question and funnel down into the specifics and you find the customer getting rather vague and perhaps a little flustered, it could be an indication that they are being rather 'economical with the truth' about the nature of the discount involved!

"It's too expensive!"

This is a phrase sales people hear many times during their selling career! This response from a customer or something similar such as "that's far too expensive" or "how much?" can mean many different things. It can mean:

- Your price is higher than one of your competitors

- Your price is cheaper than your competitor but the customer doesn't want you to know that

- Your price is within the customer's ballpark budget but they say, "its too expensive" to every sales person because when they do many sales people immediately drop their price

- Your customer may not fully understand what they are getting for the price   for instance, it is higher than another quotation they have received but that doesn't include the same level of service you are offering

So "it's too expensive" can mean many things. You need to explore this with the customer and choose an appropriate strategy to overcome their concerns over price.

Sell The Benefits Of Your Price And The Risk Associated With The Cheaper Offer

A good counter to price concerns is to demonstrate to the customer that they are very wise to pay your price. One way to do this is to highlight the risks the customer may face if they pay a cheaper price with one of your competitors. Here are some approaches to do this.

"Mr Customer, some companies provide as much as they possibly can to their customers. Whereas others provide just enough to get by. Which would you like?"

"Mr Customer, you can make a decision to pay our price just once rather than put up with poor quality forever."

"Mr Customer, we do get beaten on price. What we don't get beaten on is value for money."

"Mr Customer, any old banger will get you from A to B most of the time, but if you are looking for quality and reliability then a rusty old Ford Cortina just won't do the job!"

"Mr Customer you are absolutely right, we are more expensive than our competitors. Would you like to know why?"

"Yes you are right   it's not cheap. There are very good reasons for the price and I'd like to explain them to you."

"Mr Customer, it is a little bit more and the reason is..."

"Yes Mr Customer, it is more than some other companies and you know you always get what you pay for, don't you? Did you ever honestly buy anything cheap that was ever any good in the long run?"

"We've never been the cheapest and we are busier than ever. Would you like to know why?"

With all of the above examples, you then move back into re selling the features and benefits of your product or service and re emphasising how they solve the customer's problems, ease their pain and get them what they want.

Your aim is to convince the customer that the value of the product exceeds the price of the product. This can often be enough to handle the concern, or at the very least, lessen the reduction the customer is seeking.

Ask The Customer

This is quite a bold approach that can be very effective. In response to the customer raising a price concern, you reply:

"Mr Customer we are never the lowest price. Why do you think that even though we aren't the lowest priced supplier that so many people buy from us?"

The customer will then usually reply along the lines of quality, service and so forth. Whatever the customer offers as the reason, you respond:

"Mr Customer, you are exactly right and..." and then you can add in any additional reasons that are appropriate and move into re selling the features and benefits as described above.

Talk The Difference

In response to a customer telling you that, "You'll have to do better than that, XYZ company have offered me a much lower price!" a method to pursue is:

"Can I ask you how much cheaper?"

On many occasions the customer will tell you the price (or perhaps an even lower price than they really have been offered) and you can work out the difference between the two prices.

Then sell the benefits that the customer gets for the difference:

"Mr Customer, the difference is only £400. For that investment you get..." and sell the benefits that your product and service offers over and above the competitor.

John Ruskin

John Ruskin was a prolific writer in the 19th century. I have two of his quotes printed onto cards that I sometimes show to customers when they are attempting to haggle over price. The quotations are:

"It is unwise to pay too much, but it is unwise to pay too little. When you pay too much you lose a little money and that is all, but when you pay too little you sometimes lose everything, because the thing that you've bought isn't capable of doing the thing it was bought to do.

The common law of business prohibits you from paying a little and receiving a lot - it can't be done. If you deal with the lowest bidder it would be as well to add something for the risk you run, and if you can do that you can afford to buy something better."

"There is hardly anything in the world today that some man cannot make just a little worse and sell just a little cheaper, and the people who buy on price alone are this man's lawful prey."

> John Ruskin
> English art and social critic
> 1819 - 1900

Mr Ruskin (God bless him) has overcome many a customer price concern with his wise words. Not many people are comfortable with being someone's 'lawful prey'!

The Instant Reverse

This very bold (and somewhat cheeky) technique often shocks the customer and overcomes their price concerns. Here is how it works:

Customer: "That's expensive!"

Salesperson: "Mr Customer that is exactly the reason you should take it!"

The customer usually looks a little shocked and confused at this stage and you continue with anything that sounds logical! For example:

"You want the best value at the best price, don't you? Well you'll never get a better chance than today!"

The Trim

With this technique you lower the specification of your product and service to meet the customers price concern.

"Okay Mr Customer, it looks as if I am going to have to trim the specification to meet your price requirement. What aspects of the proposal could you do without?"

The thought of having to lose some of the benefits of your product or service is often enough for a customer to re think their price concern!

If I am discussing my fee to speak at a sales conference and the organiser attempts to drive down my price I will sometimes say:

"Okay Mr Organiser, I hear what you are saying. What most clients normally want is for me to supply some books and goodies for the audience. How would you feel if I didn't do that this time?"

If the organiser agrees then I have saved the costs of supplying the books and goodies that I would normally supply anyway, or alternatively they are concerned that they are going to miss out and agree to the original fee.

The Sweetener

Sometimes the customer wants to think they have got a better deal than the average customer, and adding something to 'sweeten the deal' can satisfy this desire.

To return to the above example, if the organiser of a sales conference is trying to drive my fee down, I could offer to run a free one or two hour seminar at the end of the afternoon, or offer a free hour of coaching for someone at the conference as a prize. This tactic of adding value is preferable to lowering my price. Let's face it, I am going to be at the venue to do my speech anyway! Adding additional value in this way can also only help my reputation!

Scratched Record

This technique is named after the tendency of the old vinyl records to jump when the playing surface is scratched and repeat the same part of the song again and again.

With the scratched record technique you just firmly and politely keep repeating your price position and the reason behind it in slightly different ways:

"The reason for the price is because of the specification, which meets your needs exactly."

"In order to give you what you really need, we need to supply the specification that costs X price."

"I appreciate your point Mr Customer however, this price guarantees our ability to give you the specification that's right for what you need."

With firmness and persistence you will be able to wear down many price concerns in this way.

Some Sales Just Aren't Worth It

The fact of the matter is that from time to time you will need to make a decision about whether some sales are worth having. Some customers are only prepared or able to spend a certain amount of money.

If after careful questioning and analysis you believe that the price the customer will buy at is below what you want, then you have a choice to make. You can choose to take the price knowing you are selling more cheaply than you ought to, or simply walk away from the order. Some sales just aren't worth it and there are many more fish in the sea!

Have confidence in yourself, your product or service and the price you charge for it and you will reap the rewards.

What You Must Always Do When You Walk Out Of The Door With An Order

Step 10 of the Bare Knuckle Selling process: "Follow Up"

Congratulations! You have closed the sale, you've won the order and you have beaten the competition! Or have you?

Now you have closed the sale this is where the real work begins. You have got to make sure that the sale goes through and that the money ends up in your bank account. I must stress that:

A sale isn't a sale until the money is in the bank!

The AA Principle

This has nothing to do with the Automobile Association or Alcoholics Anonymous! It has everything to do with keeping your customers happy and purchasing from you.

In an extensive survey consumers were asked to list what they considered the most important elements of good customer service. The top two were:

1. Availability

2. Accuracy

Availability relates to the product or service being available when the customer requires it. This not only relates to the product being physically available   on the shelf   but also to customers being able to access a service or get access to service departments and so forth. If you want to keep your customer's business then you, the relevant support people in your company and your product or service must be readily available to the customer when they want it.

Accuracy relates to the correct product or service arriving when it is supposed to arrive. The customer gets what the customer was expecting. This is doing what you said you were going to do. Not doing what you promised is just about the fastest way I know to lose sales. It also creates dissatisfaction which allows the competition to get their claws into your customer's business.

Making Your Business With Your Customers 'Bomb Proof'

If you focus upon availability and accuracy you will create a satisfied customer. Satisfied customers become loyal customers. As any salesperson can tell you, one of the hardest things to do is to get a satisfied customer to switch suppliers.

If, in addition to this, you keep close to your customer and keep up to date on their business, helping with any problems or challenges that may arise and consistently seeking to upgrade your product or service offering to them then your business with them will be almost 'bomb proof' from competitor attack. You will have effectively closed off the majority of avenues that your competitor could use to steal your business.

Complacency Kills Customer Relationships

If you maintain the correct focus on your customers and never get complacent then you will maximise your chances of a long and profitable relationship with your customer. It is estimated that it costs five times as much to find a new customer as it does to look after an existing customer. So it pays to spend a little extra time and effort with your existing customers.

A Post Call Checklist

Here are some areas for you to consider after you have closed the sale and walked out the door with the order.

Review: What Went Well?

To maximise your own learning from each and every sales call, in order to constantly improve your selling ability, it is important to always self review. Start with reviewing all of the things that went well so that you can do them again next time!

Review: What Will You Do Differently Next Time?

What aspects of the sales call were you less happy about? Did you make any mistakes? What aspects of your selling do you want to improve? We learn and improve by making mistakes and acting differently next time.

What Did You Agree To Do?

Make sure you are very clear about exactly what you have committed to do. What needs to be done next to make it happen? Who needs to take action?

Confirm Actions To The Customer In Writing

It is good selling practice to confirm specific details of each sales call you make with the customer. The customer may forget some details and written confirmation makes you appear more professional than sales people who neglect this.

In a survey of multiple grocery retailers (companies like Tesco, Asda, Wal Mart, Sainsburys etc) it was reported that only 5% of suppliers provide written confirmation of their meetings with the buyers. When you consider that multiple grocery retailers spend billions of pounds every year purchasing products, the 5% figure is quite simply staggering. This is very unprofessional and potentially financially risky. I prefer to get written confirmation to the customer promptly after every meeting.

The Japanese Samurai Principle

There is a Japanese samurai principle that says:

"After victory tighten your helmet straps"

This means that you must guard against getting complacent after you have been victorious. Once the sale has been won, put the required effort into keeping it!

So here we are at the end of the selling process. The next few chapters will give you some additional ammunition to make your competitors tremble at the mere sound of your name, you Bare Knuckle Seller you!

The Difference Between Selling & Negotiating

This is a book on selling and not on negotiation. To cover the art of negotiation would take a complete book in itself. And on that subject my book, *Bare Knuckle Negotiation*, covers the subject of how to negotiate killer deals in considerable detail. Please excuse the shameless plug but I wouldn't want to miss out on the opportunity for a sale... would you?

To be fully effective in business you need to have mastered both selling *and* negotiation. The two skills go hand in hand and it is important to understand the difference between them, and when to do each.

A Definition Of Selling

Selling can be defined as establishing a need/want to buy, and then matching the benefits of your product or service to that need/want to buy.

A Definition Of Negotiation

Negotiation can be defined as the process of bargaining to reach a mutually acceptable agreement or objective.

A Trade Unionist's Definition Of Negotiation

An experienced trade union negotiator once told me that he explained negotiation by way of a metaphor. The metaphor he used was a room with two doors. The doors are at opposite ends of the room to each other. The trade union negotiators enter the room through one door and the company management negotiators enter through the other door. Negotiation is the process of deciding where in the room the agreement is completed. Is the negotiation concluded more towards the ideal position of the company or that of the union?

I have extended this metaphor by saying that if negotiation is deciding where in the room the agreement is concluded then selling is getting people to want to come into the room in the first place!

Selling is convincing the customer that they want to buy your product or service. Negotiation is agreeing the terms on which the purchase will take place. This may include many factors such as volume purchased, delivery schedule and method, purchase frequency, amount of payment, timing of payments, advertising and marketing support and so on.

When To Sell And When To Negotiate

A simple rule of thumb to follow is to sell first and negotiate second. The reason for selling first is that the more convinced the customer is of the benefits of your product, service or proposal then the more likely they are to be prepared to pay for it! Sell first - it improves profits! If you allow yourself to be drawn into negotiation too early (as many experienced buyers will attempt to do) you are weakening your position and missing out on the opportunity to convince the customer of the benefits that your product or service brings them.

Negotiation Is The Trading Of Variables

In the process of negotiation each party (usually) trades things they *have* for things they *want* from the other party. This behaviour can be seen in the classic tussles between employers and trade unions. The trade union wants a pay increase of a specific percentage. The employer will only agree to this if the trade union agrees to some changes in working practice.

In negotiation you have to give to get. This is best done in the form of a conditional proposal: If you... Then I...

For example:

"Mr Customer if you agree to take 100 units per month then I will be able to look at the payment terms."

Sticking to the "If you... Then I..." format is good negotiation practice.

Some Negotiation Tactics To Be Aware Of

Although it is not possible to cover the full spectrum of negotiation tactics in this brief chapter, here are a few of the more dirty tactics that you may encounter.

The Salami

When you buy salami from the delicatessen, the meat is sliced in very thin slices. In negotiation a customer may attempt to salami you by securing a series of what seem to appear to be minor concessions on your part. It is only when the salami slice concessions are viewed in the totality that you realise just how much you have given away! You can counter the salami by using the "If you...Then I..." principle with every attempt at taking a slice yourself. In other words, Salami back!

The Nibble

The nibble is done when the negotiation appears to have been concluded. You have shaken hands and you think it's all over so you relax and sit back in your chair. In what appears to be an afterthought, perhaps as you are walking out of his office, the customer casually states, "That does include a free tank of petrol doesn't it?" Caught off guard many people agree. The samurai knew that after victory we have to tighten our helmet straps and they were spot on!

The counter to the nibble is to politely refuse and to state that you thought the negotiation has concluded and that if the customer wants the free tank of petrol that you will need to revisit the agreement.

"Meet Me Halfway"

This tactic involves asking the salesperson to, "meet me halfway." It appears to be very fair with each party making a concession. However, halfway is not necessarily a good place for you and the customer may have added significant amounts of 'padding' (such as telling you that they can't pay any more than £100 per unit when in fact their available budget is up to £200 per unit) to their initial position anyway. A good counter is to thank the customer for their willingness to move, and then to emphasise the fact that, due to their concession, the gap between where you and they want to conclude is now smaller. Then keep looking for ways to close this now smaller gap.

The Carrot

This is when a customer makes some promise of future benefit to you if you show flexibility this time. They'll say something like, "Help me out this time and I'll see you right next time." Unfortunately the benefit you will get is somewhat vague and it is very likely that having set the precedent this time that the same tactic will be applied in the future also. Counter this by only enhancing your proposition to the customer when you receive a specific and tangible benefit in return.

Sudden Change Of Behaviour

If a customer suddenly explodes into what appears to be an angry rage or thumps their fist down on the table in anger   stay calm. This tactic is used to shock you, to get your adrenaline flowing and to trigger the primitive fight or flight response. You can counter this by firstly recognising it as a tactic and not responding to it, and secondly by only making concessions in return for concessions of equal or greater value. If you make concessions as a result of intimidation then you are only encouraging the 'bullying' behaviour to continue.

I trust that this chapter has provided you with an insight into the vitally important skill of negotiation and how to use it in conjunction with the equally important skill of selling.

How To Get Referrals

The really great news about the Bare Knuckle Selling process is that at the end of it you end up with a satisfied customer who gets his problems solved. This is good news for getting repeat business from your customers.

The even better news is that you can use your satisfied customers to find you even more satisfied customers! You can get new customers from cold calling (which we will cover in the next chapter) but it is far easier to work from referrals.

Every single customer you have is a source of referrals. You can use your satisfied customers to introduce you to their contacts. Customers who have benefited from your product or service are usually more than happy to refer you to their colleagues, friends, family and acquaintances.

If you look at it from the customer's perspective, why wouldn't they want to recommend you? When you are a customer and you receive good service or buy a really great product you wouldn't hesitate to make a recommendation to people you know. You would want to do it because you want your family, friends or colleagues to get the same benefits that you did!

When Karen and I bought a new kitchen for our house we were delighted with the quality, service and price of the company that fitted it. They were highly professional and we are completely satisfied with the work.

Due to our recommendations we are responsible for the company fitting a further six kitchens into the houses of our friends, family and colleagues. The company didn't ask us to do this – we simply wanted to! We are not on commission (although that would be a nice idea) or any form of incentive. We want to recommend them so that people we care about can make use of a professional company too. Imagine the number of referrals that the kitchen company could get if they worked hard at it. As it is, due to their professionalism and quality they have all the work that they can cope with anyway!

Although you may receive unprompted referrals as a result of helping customers to get what they want, the wise salesperson makes securing referrals a part of their regular selling habits.

Every Customer Is A Source Of Referrals

Your customers are a gold mine of referrals, so it is worth spending some time to master the art of mining this gold.

I recommend that referral generation is done at the end of the sales call, when the customer is feeling particularly good about the decision they have made.

You need to get the customer into the right mental mind set to recall people who they can refer you to and here are some ways to do just that.

"Mr Customer, you have been in (industry/business) for many years. I guess that you have met lots of other (insert trade/position etc) haven't you? If I asked you to write down the details of four or five of these people you could do that couldn't you?"

Please not the use of "If I asked you..." The "If" softens the request. You are not directly asking him to write them down, you are merely exploring the possibility!

"Please can I ask your advice? Which one should I approach first to tell them how they can benefit?"

The customer will usually offer a name.

"It's alright to use your name so they can take my call, isn't it?"

If the customer is comfortable and receptive then you can ask for further names.

Here is an example of how I would use this to get referrals from a sales director who I had sold a programme of sales training to.

Simon: "Mr Customer, you have been a sales director over ten years haven't you? I'm guessing that you've met and know many other sales directors, don't you? If I asked you to write down the names of four or five of them you could do that, couldn't you?"

Customer: "Sure! Here you go..."

Simon: "Please can I ask your advice? Which one should I approach first so that they can get the same results you are getting from our sales training programmes?"

Customer: "Fred Jones and XYZ has a big sales force and he's in a really competitive market."

Simon: "Thanks, it's alright to use your name so Fred knows to take my call, isn't it?"

Customer: "Yeah, that's fine - say hello for me!"

Another variation that you can use is:

"Would you happen to know two or three people who might be interested in our product or service?"

The customer will usually say they know two people.

"Would you have their telephone numbers?"

The customer will usually reply yes.

"Which one would you contact first?"

The customer will tell you the name of the person, let's say his name is Bill.

"Can I ask you a huge favour? Would you call Bill and tell him I'm coming over to see him?"

This is a rather bold approach, but in the right situation it does get great results.

A slightly less bold approach is to ask the customer to write down the referral details on the back of your business card along with a personal message such as, "This product has been very useful for me."

When you get your appointment with the new prospective customer (having used the name of your existing customer who referred you) you can give them your business card as usual and then ask them to turn it over and read the message written to them on the back. This gets the sales process of to a positive start.

Referrals are an easy and effective way to get lots of new customers from your existing customers. When these new customers sign up for your product and service they, in turn, generate a new set of referrals and so the process continues.

If you find yourself doing a lot of work seeking out new customers then perhaps you aren't giving sufficient attention to getting referrals.

Cold Calling Techniques That Work

Although it can be possible to rely almost entirely upon referrals and networking to generate new customers, no book on selling would be complete without a chapter on a subject that strikes fear into the heart of even the most experienced sales person – cold calling.

Cold calling is making contact with potential customers who have never done business with you and perhaps have never even heard of you. A 'warm lead' would be from a referral where you already have 'a foot in the door'. With cold calling you don't!

It's All In The Name!

Perhaps it is the phrase 'cold calling' that bothers people. Dictionary definitions of cold include: inhospitable, unsociable, unwelcome, forbidding, unfriendly, unapproachable etc which is hardly very motivational is it?

Go On Admit It – You Are Scared!

As a Bare Knuckle Seller let's not pull any punches. Many sales people are scared of cold calling: They fear the possible (or rather inevitable) rejection and they fear appearing awkward or feeling embarrassed.

The need for acceptance and approval is buried deep in the human psyche. In primitive times if you were not accepted as part of the pack you would probably not survive. Throughout our life we seek the approval of others.

I'm Too Professional To Cold Call

Sometimes sales people tell me that they feel that cold calling is only done by sales people who are lower down the food chain than they are. They don't cold call because they are 'more professional'!

This is a load of rubbish spouted by people who just don't have the guts to cold call but are too proud to admit it.

Don't join the ranks of these wimps. You are a Bare Knuckle Seller! You have a strong desire to have lots of customers and to sell lots of stuff to them. You know what it takes. If you need more customers then you will cold call rather than sit around in the office and whine about how tough the market is.

Cold Calling Is A Safe Activity

From cold calling on guest houses in Llandudno to council estates in Leicester I have been there! I have knocked on more doors, made more cold phone calls and walked into more business reception areas than I care to remember.

On all of these occasions I have never once suffered any form of (lasting) physical injury. Cold calling is safe. The very worse that can happen is that you will be told to, "F k Off!" and have the door slammed in your face or the phone put down on you. So what?

Not a very nice experience but hardly life threatening is it? I do feel at this point I should be straight with you. I did once have to make a rapid exit from a front garden when a very large and aggressive looking Rotweiler dog appeared! Apart from that one incident, cold calling has never exposed me to any risk of harm at all.

The 'risk' from cold calling is entirely psychological in nature. It is a fear, primarily, of rejection. Indifference or initial rejection is a very common response from a pre occupied stranger. Cold calling by its nature is an interruption and sometimes, when people get interrupted, they can respond negatively.

If you look at it from the perspective of the customer, how many unsolicited telephone calls, emails, direct mail letters do they receive every month? Many of them will be from bad, pushy, talkative sales people or will be of little or no interest to the customer. Is it any wonder they may view yet another interruption negatively?

Face facts – initial negative responses come with the territory of cold calling. But they're responding negatively to the interruption and not you. You can either accept this and get on with it, or wimp out and lose sales. As a Bare Knuckle Seller you know which choice to take!

Cus D'Amato (who was Mike Tyson's boxing coach) said that, "Fear is the friend of exceptional people." High achievers are used to challenge and the fear this can sometimes bring. They expect it and welcome it. It is a sign that they are making progress.

Franklin D Roosevelt said, "The only thing we have to fear is fear itself." With that in mind let's look at how to be a success at cold calling.

The Aim of The Cold Call

What is the purpose of cold calling? The purpose is to get an appointment! The best way to sell to someone is face to face. The most effective way to get face to face is via telephone.

You need to keep this aim firmly in mind. The purpose of the initial telephone call is to *get an appointment*. Unless you are part of a focused telephone sales operation the aim of the call is not to sell your product or service. The aim of the telephone call is to get an appointment so that you can then sell face to face.

Keep focused on:

- Introducing yourself
- Introducing your company
- Arranging for an appointment

Keep these objectives in mind and do not get ahead of yourself!

The Cold Calling Process

Here are five simple steps to follow for successful cold calling:

1. Get the person's attention
2. Identify yourself and your company

3. Give the reason for your call

4. Make a qualifying/benefit statement

5. Set the appointment

Step 1: Get The Person's Attention

One of the simplest ways to get someone's attention is to use their name. You can often find out who's responsible for purchasing your specific product or service with a little research. Research can be done via directories (many specialist directories, available in your local business library, are published that give company contact details), networking, company websites or simply by asking company receptionists. If at all possible check the pronunciation and write it down phonetically. Some people get upset if their name is not pronounced correctly. I have to say that with a surname like Hazeldine I am very used to mispronunciation and misspelling and don't get offended by it, but your customer might!

A simple, "Good Morning Mr Customer" is effective as people instinctively pay attention to the sound of their own name. If you don't know how comfortable the person is with using first names then play it safe and stick to their surname.

Step 2: Identify Yourself And Your Company

Simply state your name and company and add some brief detail about your company if you choose, "This is Simon Hazeldine from E3 Group, we are a consultancy who specialise in helping companies deliver exceptional sales performance."

Step 3: Give The Reason For Your Call

You then expand upon the reason for your call and continue the process of arousing the customer's curiosity:

"The specific reason that I am calling is to set up an appointment so that I can stop by and tell you about a proven method that can increase your current sales by 10 to 20%."

Another variation that you can use is:

"The special reason that I am calling today is to show you a new idea that several other (insert type of company) companies like yours tell us is resulting in sales increases of up to 20%."

Note the use of words such as 'specific', 'special' and 'idea'. These are all designed to increase the customer's curiosity.

A further variation on this step is to say:

"The specific reason that I am calling is that we specialise in sales training and increasing sales for our clients and I thought I'd give you a call to see if you would be interested in chatting through the various options available. Is increasing your sales success through training something you've given much thought to?"

It doesn't really matter what they answer as you can then move onto making a qualifying benefit statement and securing an appointment!

Step 4: Make A Qualifying/Benefit Statement

The aim of this step is to tantalise and to stir up enough interest and curiosity to make them want to see you.

You need to answer the customer's unspoken question, "Why should I listen to you?" and cause them to wonder, "What is it all about?"

It is important to guard against them pre judging your product or service without you seeing them. Don't give too much away! Pre judgement is one of the biggest problems you can encounter when cold calling. Tell them enough to arouse curiosity but no more.

You can say:

"Mr Customer, I am sure that you, like a lot of the companies we work with (if you have some high profile clients you can insert some specific examples), want increased sales, don't you?"

or

"Mr Customer several of our other clients such as (insert name/names of clients) tell me that this new method helps their sales people to increase sales by up to 20%. I guess you'd be interested in that, wouldn't you?"

or

"Mr Customer, I was wondering if you would be interested in a proven method that can increase your sales by 20% in the next 12 months?"

Please note the use of tag questions to elicit a positive response to your statement. It all helps!

Step 5: Set The Appointment

Now it is time to close on the appointment.

"That's great Mr Customer, then we should get together. How about Tuesday at 3.30 pm?"

or

"Mr Customer you could evaluate this idea in about 20 minutes. How about Tuesday at 3.30pm?"

or

"Mr Customer I would just need about 20 minutes to show you what I've got and then you can judge it for yourself."

You can also use the 'alternative close' effectively in this situation:

"How about Monday at 3.30pm or would some time on Tuesday be better?"

Asking for appointments on the half hour (3.30pm) mentally reserves half an hour (and not a full hour) in the customer's mind. This firstly makes it easier for them to fit you into their schedule and secondly reduces the risk of cancellation.

Things Not To Say

I dislike being contacted by cold callers who say things like:

"This is just a courtesy call." No it isn't   it's a sales call and the customer knows it is! Is pretending to be making a 'courtesy call' likely to inspire trust from a potential customer?

Other phrases to avoid are:

"Can I have a few minutes of your time?" Likely to elicit a response of, "No you can't!"

"Sorry to disturb you, but..." If you are sorry about disturbing me then why did you call in the first place?

"Is this a bad time?" Now you come to mention it, "Yes it is!"

"I'm just calling on businesses in your sector..." That doesn't make the customer feel very special does it?

"We are calling to conduct a survey." And following the survey, surprise, surprise they have a product or service to sell you. Once the customer realises that the 'survey' was just a ploy to get information from them, and set them up to be sold to, that you've already lost their trust. Not a good start for a sales call.

Avoid phrases such as these and stick to the process outlined previously. It is tested, proven and effective.

An alternative and refreshingly different (and honest) approach is one utilised by my good friend Jamie Smart who runs a very successful NLP training and consultancy company. When he cold calls he says, "Hi Mr Customer, This is Jamie Smart calling from Salad Consulting. This is a sales call, and I'll need about 1 minute of your time. Is now a good time to talk?" Typically Jamie finds that the customer either says "Yes" or tells him a time that would be better. It is an honest, bold and effective approach.

Be Bold!

I appreciate that much of this process will seem rather bold. To be effective at cold calling you need to be! You are a Bare Knuckle Seller. You are a sales professional who's product or service delivers genuine benefit to your customers. As good as your product or service is, you are likely to be operating in a competitive market and need to be bold in order to get yourself in front of customers ahead of your competition.

Possible Customer Responses
And What To Do With Them

Broadly speaking there are five possible customer responses at this stage of the cold call:

1. "We are not interested"

2. "We already have a supplier for that"

3. "Just put something in the post to me"

4. "Just tell me about it now"

5. "Give me a call next week"

The first two responses can be dealt with by using a variation on the 'feel, felt, found' approach to handling customer concerns discussed earlier. For example:

"We are not interested."

"I understand how you feel, a lot of my clients told me the same thing before they had a chance to see exactly how X benefited them."

or

"I didn't think you'd be interested and that's why I'm calling you (this unusual approach hooks the customer's attention superbly). Almost every single client who is now using our services was also initially not interested."

"We already have a supplier."

"I understand how you feel Mr Customer. A lot of people have told me that same thing before they had a chance to see how what we do fits/matches/compliments/enhances what their existing supplier is doing."

These two responses are managed by using a variation on 'feel, felt, found' structure:

"I understand how you <u>feel</u> Mr Customer, several of my clients who are now benefiting from our unique sales training method <u>felt</u> exactly the same way until they <u>found</u> that our cutting edge process resulted in sales increases of up to 20%."

Then go back to closing for an appointment!

"Just tell me about it now."

This can be handled as follows:

"Mr Customer, I wish I could tell you all about it in a word or two. You will be able to evaluate it a lot faster by seeing it. It would take just 20 minutes for you to determine if it is right for you."

or

"Mr Customer I'd love to tell you, however because I have something that I have to show you I need to see you in person. It will take me about 15 to 20 minutes and then you can decide for yourself. Hundreds of companies are using it, it's a great success, so why don't you see for yourself? Would you have 20 minutes free this week?"

Please note the use of the word "because" in the previous paragraph. The word "because" is a very powerful word for Bare Knuckle Sellers to be aware of.

Experiments by social psychologist Ellen Langer revealed that when we ask someone to so something we will be far more successful if we provide a reason. People like to have reasons for what they do.

Langer demonstrated the power of this fact in experiments with a photocopying machine in a library.

When attempting to jump the queue to use the photocopier by saying, "Excuse me, I have five pages. May I use the photocopier?", only 60% of people complied.

However, when Langer said, "Excuse me, I have five pages. May I use the photocopies <u>because</u> I am in a rush?" a staggering 94% of people let her skip ahead of them in the queue!

You may think that the reason people let Langer go ahead of them was the justification of her being in a rush. However a third type of request showed that this was not the case.

When Langer said, "Excuse me, I have five pages. May I use the photocopying machine <u>because</u> I need to make some copies?" a staggering 93% of people complied with her request.

The word "because" appears to be the 'trigger word' that fired off *an automatic compliance response!* I am sure that you can find many uses for this technique because it is highly influential!

If the customer continues to push for more detail then continue to raise their curiosity by placing emphasis on what your product or service will do rather than a description of it. Then close for an appointment.

"Just put something in the post for me."

Things that are posted in this way usually end up being filed in the bin or spend several weeks lurking under a pile of paper on the customer's desk before being thrown away. Literature is to be left after your sales call and not sent in advance! Be bold and say:

"I really prefer not to post anything, can we get together next Tuesday at 3.30pm?"

Another approach is to say,

"Mr Customer I'm in your area this week, I'll drop it off personally. Will you be there?" This really helps to flush out if they are interested or not!

"Give me a call next week."

This can often just be a put off and can be handled by being bold and saying:

"Mr Customer, I have my diary here, is yours handy? Why don't we set a time right now."

Referring back to the section on embedded suggestions will enable you to make the most of embedding the suggestion, "set a time right now!"

Alternatively, if it is genuinely not a good time for the potential customer then set a specific time to call back. When you do call back say:

"Mr Customer this is Simon Hazeldine from E3 Group, you specifically asked me to call back after the weekend to set up an appointment. Would Tuesday at 3.30pm be good for you?"

Getting Past Gatekeepers

In today's modern business world access to many key decision makers is via their secretaries or PAs. Although I am a sales person by profession my secretary is instructed to shield me from the many approaches I receive every week from sales people.

At first this may seem somewhat hypocritical on my part. However, when you consider that I, like many other people, have my own business and customers to attend to, you will understand that if I spent my time answering every sales enquiry received that I would not be able to focus on what is important to me.

So the first important point is to understand that the customer is not being deliberately difficult. It is just that due to the volume of unsolicited telephone calls, sales calls, direct mail and emails received every week along with all the meetings to attend, messages to return, deadlines to meet, customers to look after, various business projects to manage and families to get home to at a reasonable time, that customers will shield themselves from unsolicited interruption.

Secondly, the receptionist, secretary or PA is just doing their job. They have probably been told to screen out unsolicited telephone calls from sales people. They might even get into trouble if they let too many 'annoying' phone calls through to their boss.

I actually view this as a positive advantage. Sales people who don't know how to cope with this barrier will be unsuccessful in penetrating through to the decision maker. This leaves the field clear for those of us who do!

First, Get Your Attitude Sorted!

One of the secrets of successful cold calling is to have to right attitude. You are not a timewaster or a pesky salesperson.

You are a professional person who has products, services ideas, information and expertise that will be valuable to the right customer. You are a knowledgeable expert in your field. Your business is just as legitimate as the customer's business. Your time is just as important to you as their time is to them. They are no more important than you are.

Add to this attitude an air of authority and purpose and you will be unstoppable!

Here are a number of techniques that you can use to get past gatekeepers you authoritative, professional sales expert, you!

Remind Them Of Their Job

Being bold and using an authoritative tone can sometimes be enough:

"Please connect me with Mr Customer, thank you."

As mentioned previously a downward voice inflection signals a command that will often be obeyed! Use this when saying the above.

Please note the use of the word "thank you". Thank you is rather like "because". It is a trigger word. "Thank you" when used in this way often triggers an automatic response to put you through!

You will often be asked what your call is about to which you can reply:

"It's about a conversation, thank you." It could of course be a conversation you are *about* to have with the prospective customer!

Or you could say:

"It's about our correspondence, thank you." You could use this is you were following up on a mail shot for example.

Get One Step Ahead

Some customers instruct their secretary to always say they are out when receiving calls from sales people. If this happens a few times with a customer you can get one step ahead so they can't keep doing this to you!

Salesperson: "Is Mr Customer there?"

Secretary: "Who's calling?"

Salesperson: "Is he there?"

Secretary: "Yes"

Gotcha! At the very least you now know that he is in!

What's It In Connection With?

If a secretary asks this question you can respond:

"It's in connection with sales training, he does deal with sales training doesn't he? Can you put me through, thank you."

or

"It's something I can only discuss with Mr Customer, will you put me through please, thank you."

Off Peak

Many people arrive in the office before their secretary and stay working after their secretary has gone home. In these situations, because they are not expecting many, if any calls, they will answer their phone themselves. Before 9am and after 5pm can be open season to get straight through to decision makers.

I discovered this technique when I was calling to arrange an appointment with the CEO of a massive company. The company had an annual turnover of hundreds of millions of pounds. I phoned at approximately 5.30pm hoping to speak to the CEO's PA who managed his diary. To my surprise the CEO answered his PA's direct line and I made the appointment on the spot. Ever since then, when

I am 'big game hunting' (bagging appointments with CEOs and the like) I start calling early or late in the day with superb results!

Leaving Messages On Voicemail

When cold calling I prefer not to leave voicemail messages if at all possible, however sometimes it can become necessary to do so.

I have two formats, the second being a rather bolder approach!

The first approach is to follow the this structure:

1. Customer name: "Hello Mr Customer"
2. My Name: "This is Simon Hazeldine from E3 Group"
3. My telephone number
4. Tantalise and stir up: "I'm calling to discuss how companies in the X industry are using a unique method and increasing their sales by 20%." or "I'm calling to discuss an innovative approach to raising your sales by between 10 and 20%."
5. My telephone number (again)
6. State what I want them to do: "Please call me tomorrow so that we can talk further."

This approach usually proves effective.

The second, bolder approach is to say:

"Mr Customer this is Simon Hazeldine from E3 Group, my number is X, they said you were the right person to..." and then I hang up!

The customer usually thinks that their machine has cut of the phone call and in approximately 90% of cases they'll return the call.

Leaving Messages With Secretaries

A bold and somewhat cheeky format for leaving a message is:

1. Your name
2. Your company
3. Your telephone number
4. Say it is regarding another company known to the customer

5. And add, "He'll know."

This provokes curiosity and when the customer calls you can refer to the other company and how they are using your product or service.

Some of these techniques are rather bold and require nerve but they are effective in getting you through to decision makers and getting your calls returned.

Cold Calling In Person

You can adapt many of the techniques discussed for phone calls when cold calling in person. You can always find opportunities to cold call in person. One easy way is to cold call on companies in the same building or on the same industrial estate as your customer. You can always ask your customer if they know the people in the next building or office. They often do and can help with a referral.

It is important to adopt an air of purpose and authority and positively stride up to the receptionist! If you know the person's name confidently state:

"Mr Customer, thank you."

or

"Is Mr Customer in?"

If they ask you if you have an appointment say:

"That's why I'm calling, please tell Mr Customer I'm here, thank you."

If they ask what it is in relation to, reply:

"I specialise in seeing people in the XYZ industry and I want to see Mr Customer is he in?"

If they ask what you are selling, decline to comment by saying;

"I'm from XYZ company, kindly tell Mr Customer I'm here to see him."

Don't rely on charm, that's what the average sales person does! When cold calling be bold, be assertive and keep persisting. Most receptionists will put a call through to the person you are seeking.

I have also enjoyed success with this approach:

"I know you've never met me before and I know your boss is a busy person and I also know that because I have something that will help him with his business that he would want you to give me an opportunity to talk to him."

Note the use of true pacing statements ("you've never met me before" and "your boss is a busy person"), the use of because, the use of the bosses authority ("he would want you to") and the embedded suggestion ("give me an opportunity to talk to him").

Another variation is:

"I know what your job is like, I have a secretary. I know it's difficult for you to know who to let him speak to but because I do have something of great importance, I know he will appreciate you letting him see it. Would you please tell him I'm here?"

If your job title is at all impressive then this perceived authority can help to tip the balance in your favour with receptionists. Striding in wearing your smartest suit, with an air of authority and saying something like, "Good morning, Simon Hazeldine – I'm the Managing Director of E3 Group and I'm here to see Mr Customer." will often result in the receptionist contacting the person you are seeing immediately!

Cold calling should be treated as a challenge. Even with these great techniques you won't get through every time! Keep persisting. It's understandable to dislike rejection – just don't get discouraged or defeated by it. By being mentally tough you will get through to more prospective customers than your competitors can. This means more sales for you!

The Rules Of Bare Knuckle Selling Revisited

So here we are at the end of the book! Along the way you have been exposed to some of the most effective, cutting edge sales techniques and strategies available.

Following the Bare Knuckle Selling process will put you into the top 1% of sales people on the planet because it is based upon proven and effective methods.

Let's just recap the steps of the Bare Knuckle Selling Process because they are the steps you need to take to reach the very top of the selling profession:

Before the sales call

Step 1: Plan and Prepare
Step 2: Set SMASH objectives and get into a "Top Ten State"

During the sales call

Step 3: Introduce, Hook and get Rapport
Step 4: Understand customer needs and criteria
Step 5: Understand the customer's budget
Step 6: Get the agreement to proceed
Step 7: Propose and Present
Step 8: Reinforce needs, criteria and solutions
Step 9: Secure the result

After the sales call

Step 10: Follow Up

Please ensure that you commit these steps and their accompanying techniques and tactics to memory. Make them your own, adapt them to suit your personal style and then... leave your competitors choking in your dust!

The Three Rules Of Bare Knuckle Selling Revisited

Let us now review the three rules that we explored at the start of this book:

Rule 1: Your customers (and customers to be) are not stupid.

As we know, people are becoming more educated, more sophisticated, better informed, and far more discerning. People don't fall for blatant and manipulative tactics anymore they resent them and the people who use them.

The successful sales person of the future must treat their customers and customers to be with respect. In this way they will be respected themselves.

Rule 2: Sell how you like to be sold to

People like to be treated with respect and courtesy. People like to be listened to. People like the sales person to be interested in finding out what they want. People want the sales person to put their interests first. People want to be helped to make a decision that is right for them.

Attempting to sell any other way is basically rather stupid. Why would anyone who knows what they are doing, attempt to sell using out dated manipulative methods?

Bare Knuckle Sellers always sell in the way that they would like to be sold to.

As a result they close more sales and build far more stable, long term customer relationships.

Rule 3: Sell only to people who need what you've got.

People are convinced that sales people want to sell them something. They are right, so tell them what 'you're up to'...

The antidote to people's fears and concerns about sales people is to tell them what you are doing.

The Bare Knuckle Seller tells people up front that their company exists by engaging in commercial transactions or relationships with customers. You provide products and/or services to customers and they pay money for them.

What separates the Bare Knuckle Seller is what you do first. The most important thing you do is to understand what is important to the prospective customer. When you understand this, you will see if your products and/or services can truly help them.

If they can, then you will recommend an appropriate solution. The customer can then decide to say "yes" or "no" to the proposal. Being up front with the customer you demonstrate how different you are from the herd of manipulative sales people, remove customer fears and establish trust with them.

Good Luck And Good Selling

All that remains is to wish to the very best success with all of your selling. I firmly believe that you make your own luck in life and mastering the art of Bare Knuckle Selling will make you one of the 'luckiest' sales people around.

We are fortunate to live in a prosperous and abundant universe. There has never been as much wealth and prosperity in society as there is now. As Richard Bandler (the co creator of NLP) has said, "Once there was no money in the world and now look how much there is." Rather than just hoping for more wealth and bemoaning your lot, you need to open up a channel to receive it. I shall close with a story that illustrates this point.

There was once a man who ended up in debt and as a result of his consistent borrowing his debts grew and grew. Finally in desperation he went to his local church to plead for mercy.

The first week he went to the church and prayed, "Please God, please, please, please let me win the lottery. If I could just win the lottery all of my problems will be solved." Nothing happened.

The second week he went back to church and feeling even more desperate prayed again, "Look God you've got to help me out. My debts are growing, I can't think of anything to do. Please, please, please you've got to make me win the lottery." Again nothing happened.

The third week he almost crawled back to church feeling at his wits end. He threw himself on the floor at the altar and with tears streaming down his face shouted out aloud, "God what the hell are you doing? Can't you see how desperate and wretched I am? If you have any compassion at all, please, please, please let me win the lottery or I haven't a hope left."

All of a sudden there was a loud clap of thunder and a bolt of lightning. The man suddenly heard God's voice booming out from heaven. God said to the man:

"I'm listening, I'm listening. Help me out here, meet me halfway! At least buy a lottery ticket!"

Being exceptional at the art and science of selling will allow you to open up a channel to the wealth and prosperity that surrounds us all in our modern society.

Meet the abundant universe you live in halfway – become a master of selling!

About The Author

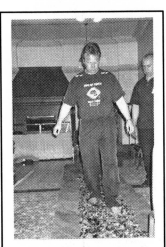

Simon Hazeldine demonstrates his mental focus by walking barefoot over a twenty foot bed of razor sharp broken glass!

Simon Hazeldine MSc, FInstSMM

"...a hard hitting speaker who will give you a wake up call that you'll never forget!"

Simon Hazeldine is a recognised expert in the fields of:

- The Psychology of Performance
- The Psychology of Influence
- Selling and Negotiation

Simon writes a monthly column on the psychology of performance in four national magazines and is the author of:

"Bare Knuckle Selling", "Bare Knuckle Negotiation", "The Winner's Edge: Psychological Strategies for Exceptional Performance" and a series of eight psychological training guides for martial artists and sportspeople.

Simon works internationally as a speaker, trainer, coach and facilitator in the areas of performance, leadership, sales, negotiation and influential communication.

His "High Performance Coaching Skills", "Group Training Techniques" and "Negotiation Skills" programmes are currently being used in 28 countries around the world.

Simon has a Masters Degree in the psychology and management of performance. In addition he is Certified as a Master Practitioner and Trainer of NLP, and is a Fellow of the Institute of Sales and Marketing Management.

Simon has extensive experience in sales both in the UK and abroad and has been responsible for numerous client accounts each worth in excess of £20 million in sales. Prior to his career as a trainer and speaker Simon provided event security and personal protection services to celebrities in the television and music industry.

Simon Hazeldine's acclaimed keynote speeches include:

"How To Raise Your Game", "How To Get What You Want By Being Selfish and Unreasonable", "Are You Tough Enough? The 7 Secrets of Mental Toughness", "How To Find Your Customers G Spot", "How To Hurt Your Competitors Using Bare Knuckle Selling"

To initially receive a good listening to please contact Simon at:

Email: simon@simonhazeldine.com

Bibliography

Andreas, Steve & Faulkner, Charles, *NLP: The New Technology of Achievement*, Nicholas Brealey Publishing 1996

Bandler, Richard & La Valle, John, *Persuasion Engineering*, Meta Publications 1996

Bandler, Richard & Grinder, John, *Patterns of the Hypnotic Techniques of Milton H. Erickson, M.D Volume 1*, Meta Publications 1975

Bandler, Richard & Grinder, John, *Patterns of the Hypnotic Techniques of Milton H. Erickson, M.D Volume 2*, Meta Publications 1977

Cialdini, Robert, *Influence*, Harper Collins College Publishers 1993

Fenton, John, *Close! Close! Close!*, Mercury Business Books 1990

Harvey, Christine, *Secrets of the World's Top Sales Performers*, Business Books Limited 1989

Hazeldine, Simon, *The Winner's Edge: Psychological Strategies for Exceptional Performance*, Winner's Edge Publications 2004

Jenkins, Debbie & Gregory, Joe: *The Gorillas Want Bananas: The Lean Marketing Handbook for Small Expert Businesses*, Lean Marketing Press 2001

Rackham, Neil, *Spin Selling*, Gower 1995

Smart, Jamie, *Irresistible Influence Cards*, Wordsalad Publications 2003

McKenna, Paul and Breen Michael, *The Power To Influence* (Audio), Nightingale Conant

Smart, Jamie, *Ethical Influence with NLP* (Audio), Wordsalad Publications 2004

Tracy, Brian, *The Psychology of Selling* (Audio), Nightingale Conant

Want Some More?

**Book Simon Hazeldine as a Keynote Speaker
for your Conference or Event**

*"...a hard hitting speaker who will give you a
wake up call that you'll never forget!"*

Keynote speeches include:

- *"How to get what you want by being selfish and unreasonable"*
- *"How to hurt your competitors with Bare Knuckle Selling"*
- *"How to raise your game"*
- *"Are you tough enough? The 7 secrets of mental toughness"*

Further information on Simon's keynote speeches can be obtained
from his Professional Speakers Association webpage:

www.professionalspeakers.org/members/SimonHazeldine

E3 Group: Inspiring and Enabling Exceptional Performance

*"The E3 Group provides consultancy and training that delivers
significant sales and business performance enhancement"*

The unique E3 Group approach is based on ensuring that you have
the three essential factors that guarantee on going sales success
hard wired into your organisation.

Highly effective solutions will be specifically designed, tailored and
delivered in house to meet your specific requirements.

Examples of training solutions provided by the E3 Group include:

- Sales Skills Training
- Advanced Sales Skills Training
- Negotiation Skills Training
- Cold Calling Skills Training
- Coaching Skills for Managers and Leaders
- Effective Sales Management
- Effective Performance Management

- Developing Superior Customer Relationships
- Selling with NLP
- The Psychology of Persuasion and Influence
- Key Account Management and National Account Management training
- Public Speaking and Presentation Skills
- The Psychology of Exceptional Performance
- Developing Mental Toughness
- Performance Leadership

The E3 Group also offers a series of open programmes:

- **The Bare Knuckle Selling Bootcamp:** 2 day open programme that will teach you how to be a bare knuckle seller!

- **The Bare Knuckle Negotiation Bootcamp:** 2 day open programme that will give you the winning edge

- **Advanced Selling Workshop:** 2 day open programme on the psychology of persuasion and influence

- **Psychology of Performance Workshop:** 2 day open programme that will reveal the real psychological strategies and techniques used by elite performers

- **I Will!:** 1 day motivation and peak performance seminar with Simon Hazeldine. Break through limiting beliefs, take control of your life, discover your simple single truth and raise your game to new heights.

To book Simon as your speaker or to find out more about E3 Group's services and courses contact Simon Hazeldine:

The E3 Group
1 Dexter Close
Quorn
Loughborough
Leicestershire
LE12 8EH
United Kingdom

Email: simon@simonhazeldine.com

Printed in the United Kingdom
by Lightning Source UK Ltd.
129512UK00001B/327/A